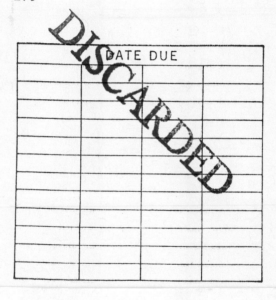

TWAYNE'S WORLD AUTHORS SERIES
A Survey of the World's Literature

YUGOSLAVIA

EDITOR OF THIS VOLUME

John Loud, Texas Christian University

Antun Gustav Matoš

TWAS 635

Antun Gustav Matoš

ANTUN GUSTAV MATOŠ

By EUGENE E. PANTZER

TWAYNE PUBLISHERS

A DIVISION OF G. K. HALL & CO., BOSTON

Published in 1981 by Twayne Publishers,
A Division of G. K. Hall & Co.
All Rights Reserved

Printed on permanent/durable acid-free paper and bound
in the United States of America

First Printing

Library of Congress Cataloging in Publication Data

Pantzer, Eugene E
Autun Gustav Matoš.

(Twayne's world authors series ; TWAS 635)
Bibliography: p. 136
Includes index.
1. Matoš, Antun Gustav, 1873–1914.   2. Authors,
Croatian—20th century—Biography.
PG1618.M35Z79   891.8′28409 [B]   80-29499
ISBN 0-8057-6478-X

Contents

About the Author

Eugene Pantzer is a Middle Westerner who was transplanted early to the East. Born in Sheboygan, Wisconsin, he attended school in Massachusetts. He is a graduate of Harvard, where he received a doctorate in Slavic and Oriental languages. After a career in government service and college teaching (Georgetown, George Washington, New England College), he now lives on a farm in central New Hampshire, when not traveling or doing research.

Preface

Outside Croatia, the name Matoš is virtually unknown. That is a pity, for the situation deserves to be changed. Storyteller, poet, essayist, and critic, Matoš struck out in various directions—to the delight (and frequently to the dismay) of his contemporaries. His literary manner has been celebrated; although, in general, the effect of his wit depends too often on partisan and regional affiliations. Matoš really goes beyond the mere literary wight or Croatian patriot: he is interesting as a personality; as a man of contradictions (some of them great); as an embattled and argumentative soul who, even today, cannot quite be forgotten.

In his own land he matters *historically* (if that word does not frighten away the innocent; is not everything *in* history, though not necessarily magnified into greatness by the fact?). Matoš got about. Although a Croat, he also lived in Serbia, Germany, Switzerland, and France. He experienced turn-of-the-century Europe as the first Yugoslav Bohemian. (The part of a dandy was preferable, but was out of reach.) Well-read, articulate, he earnestly attempted to transplant what he understood of French literary standards to his backward homeland; he wanted to permute foreign culture into a South Slavic mode. A professional writer at a time when there were few others, he thus represents a new and sophisticated viewpoint which appealed to the younger Yugoslav generation.

If that is insufficient, consider this: Matoš lived during a fascinating time. His Yugoslavia was beset by the problems of a rising industrial middle class and by factionalism (ethnic as well as political). Croats and Serbs hated each other, yet both in common detested Hungarians and Austrians. He lived in Europe of the Belle Epoque and tasted its delights: the Paris Exposition of 1900; neo-romanticism; late impressionism; his were the closing years of an age before the world's fabric was irretrievably torn. Here is Matoš taking notes, writing letters from abroad—a vivid (if not objective) reporter of what was happening around him, in forever impecunious circumstances.

He hurries onward, like Zeno's arrow, while the weary biographer invariably lags him by one station, at the least. Even with film and camera, the pursuer can only provide a few "stills," without conveying the liveliness and movement. Since mine is the limited treatment of a difficult subject, I have focused on broad aspects which might appeal to readers unacquainted with Yugoslav literature. Matoš ought to speak for himself. In what follows he will be quoted liberally, sometimes to his detriment.

What emerges? My portrait makes of him an exile, an alien, someone *in* but not *of* his time. Matoš chimes with very little, wherever he happens to be. That essentially negative view of him may not sit well with his countrymen, but it is the way American readers will, I believe, best understand what this difficult man is all about.

For difficult he is, in word and deed. Yugoslav editors feel obliged to gloss him, even for his present-day readers at home. In these circumstances, good guides are necessary and, fortunately, are available. Dragutin Tadijanović has assembled a *Sabrana djela* [Collected Works] which is a model of its kind, a compendium which makes all else possible. Also to be mentioned are scholars like Velibor Gligorić, Tode Čolak, and Olga Grahor. In the end, of course, the difficulties come home to roost. A patient wife, Irene, has lived with my frustrations. A sometimes demonic editor named John Loud has kept reading and rereading the manuscript, trying to match sense and sensibility. A benign mentor, Albert Lord, has smiled afar down the Harvard Olympus. All deserve profound thanks. Let me add that I also benefited greatly from conversations with Davor Kapetanić, an editor of Matoš's notebooks and letters.

EUGENE PANTZER

Last Legs, New Hampshire

Chronology

1873 Antun Matoš born at Tovarnik in Srem (a district northwest of Belgrade) on Friday, 13 June, the second of five children of August Matoš and Maria Schams.

1875 Family moves to Zagreb and after several relocations, settles at 10 Jurjevska in Gornji Grad, a section of the city.

1883 Antun becomes a gymnasium student; completes seven grades, with an intermittent flyer in music school (where he fails theory). Spends vacations with the Ante Pinterović family in rural Brezovica.

1889 While still at the gymnasium, he writes first work: a sonnet to sweetheart Dragica Tkalčić.

1891 Spends fall semester at veterinary school in Vienna; but falls ill, flunks exams, loses scholarship.

1892 Publishes "Power of Conscience," first story, in Zagreb periodical *Vijenac*.

1893 Drafted into cavalry; sent to horse-breeding station at Kutjevo (in Slavonia).

1894 Transferred to farrier's school in Zagreb during June, he deserts in August. After visiting Tovarnik, he heads for Serbia, but is arrested at Mitrovica and imprisoned. Escapes and finally reaches Belgrade by October; is refused permission to continue studies.

1895 Becomes journalist, begins keeping notebooks.

1896 Engaged as cellist in Royal Serbian National Theater. Now adds middle name "Gustav" to his signature.

1898 Leaves Belgrade for Budapest, Vienna, Munich, and Geneva. Visits uncle Dr. Ferdinand Schams near Vienna.

1899 *Iverje* [Chips], first story collection, published in Mostar. August, leaves Geneva for Paris. November, grandfather Grgur Matoš dies.

1900 April, starts to write *Dojmovi sa pariške izložbe* [Impressions of the Paris Exposition]. Meets André Rouveyre, artist and friend. *Novo iverje* [Fresh Chips], second collection of stories, published in Zagreb.

1903   Receives letter with money from Olga Herak, later to be his fiancée.

1904   Returns to Belgrade.

1905   Arthritis becomes painful. Twice secretly visits Zagreb. *Ogledi* [Perspectives], essays, published in Zadar.

1906   "Consolation from Her Tress" in *Savremenik* is first poem intended for publication. Visits Croatia a third time.

1907   Yet again visits Zagreb. *Vidici i putovi* [Look-outs and High Roads] appears in Zagreb.

1908   Amnestied; returns to Zagreb for good; travels around Croatia. Writes "Za Kranjčevića" [For Kranjčević].

1909   Last story collection published: *Umorne priče* [Tales from Melancholy]. Passes examination qualifying him as high school teacher of French.

1910   *Naši ljudi i krajevi* [Our People at Home], selected critical essays.

1911   Medical visit to Italy (Florence, Venice).

1912   Publishes *Dragi naši savremenici* [Our Dear Contemporaries]. Visits Rijeka and seacoast area.

1913   Last visit to Italy (Rome). *Pečalba* [Day Labor], final book, appears. Enters hospital, terminally ill.

1914   Undergoes further surgery. Dies on Thursday, 17 March. Buried in Mirogoj cemetery.

CHAPTER 1

Life and Times

MATOŠ'S lifetime (1873–1914) fell between the Franco-Prussian War and World War I. In retrospect, this was a time of great material and technological progress, when world population and industrial output increased, when weaponry became more destructive—a time when the threads of European civilization still hung together, if more loosely; a time of "soft air" which later journalists, like Walter Lippmann, were glad to remember.[1] All in all, it was an Age of Progress preceding the Decline of the West.

From Matoš's viewpoint, however, the momentousness of the age was not so apparent. The federated Kingdom of Serbs, Croats, and Slovenes did not exist before 1918; Yugoslavia, before 1929; and the six federated republics, before World War II. The immediate realities were Serbia and Croatia.

Serbia, under Turkish rule since the Battle of Kosovo (1389), had gained a measure of self-government as the result of revolts led, first by the pig-merchant Karađorđe (1805–1813), then by Miloš Obrenović (1815–1817). The success or failure of these efforts depended ultimately upon Russia, foe of the Turk and defender of the Orthodox brethren. Until 1815 Russia was much occupied with Napoleon Bonaparte, who himself gave impetus to national liberation fronts.

When Miloš won recognition as hereditary prince of the Belgrade *pashalik*, he had his Karađorđe rival slain. A feud between the two families lasted until 1903, when the Obrenović line came to a bloody end. It was a turbulent time: there were no less than eight changes of rule between 1815 and 1903.[2] Still, by 1861 the last Turkish garrison had left Belgrade and institutions like the University of Belgrade and the Academy of Sciences had appeared. The Serbia of Matoš's time seemed well along the road to autonomy.

Another Serbian development was nationalism. Patriotic organizations like the *Omladina* ("Homeland") sprouted everywhere after 1848, in the context of a romantic movement, still potent in the Bal-

11

kans, calling for individualism and self-expression. The persevering efforts of Vuk Stefanović Karadžić (1787–1864) to establish a national language based on popular speech also looked in that direction.

Milan Obrenović (reigned 1868–1889) erred by declaring war on the Ottoman Empire (1876). Russia intervened to help the Serbs, it is true. Yet the Congress of Berlin (1878) revealed that Russia cared more about Bulgaria. Nor did Austrian occupation of Bosnia-Hercegovina, an immediate consequence of the Congress, make the Serbs any happier; this province (which Austria later formally annexed, in 1908), more or less divided Serbia from Croatia.

Milan never imagined a Bismarck or a Garibaldi, either. But the net effect of their achievements was fateful for his little kingdom: "The 1860's brought about the unification of Germany and Italy, areas over which Austria had once exerted a large measure of control. Forced out of central Europe, Vienna could only turn southward."[3] After Milan's successor, Alexander (reigned 1889–1903), was murdered by anti-Austrian conspirators, Petar Karađorđević (1903–1921) realigned Serbia on a collision course. The collision occurred on 28 June 1914 when the Archduke Franz Ferdinand's assassination brought on a world war.

Croatia's autonomy was purely internal. Squeezed between the Venetian Republic and Hungary, Croatia surrendered independence in favor of Hungarian overlordship (1102). The Hungarian king was represented by a viceroy or *ban*, who resided in Zagreb. Although still enjoying a small amount of domestic freedom, Croatia became part of a larger political entity for more than eight hundred years.

The nineteenth century brought new joys and disappointments. Napoleon fed liberationist hopes by incorporating the Illyrian Provinces with land taken from Austria and Venice. But in 1815 the Napoleonic structure was dismantled, and further downward changes were in store. During the stormy days of 1848 the Croats moved against Hungary. *Ban* Jelačić mounted an invasion which succeeded only with Russian help. Then he combined forces with the authoritarian Prince Windischgrätz to force out the old emperor in Vienna. The new ruler, Franz Joseph I (1848–1916), barely eighteen, wasted no tears on vanquished Hungarians and had little time for revolutionaries. His own conservatism was expressed in the "Bach System" of Austrification. During the years that followed Croatia functioned virtually as an Austrian province.

Soon, however, the Hapsburgs were brought up short by nationality problems. In 1867 a division into Austrian Empire and Hungarian

Kingdom accommodated Magyar pressures. Franz Joseph remained ruler, and there was a single voice in foreign, military, and financial affairs. But elsewhere the two domains became separate. In the Balkans, Dalmatia and Slovenia were ruled by Austria; Croatia (including Slavonia and the Vojvodina), by Hungary.

Once more the Magyars had risen to a position of strength and governed accordingly; Magyarization was the order of the day. Much friction ensued, all very familiar to Matoš. Indeed, the twenty-year *ban*-ship of Count Karl Khuen Héderváry began in 1883. The young Matoš, who often saw him strolling to the Cmrok park, once very nearly got the entire family arrested with his catcalling.[4] In 1894 the citizens of Zagreb publicly desecrated a Hungarian flag during Franz Joseph's visit. The repressions which followed influenced many young students toward cities like Prague, where the atmosphere was more liberal.

Croatia posed a problem to the empire. Not that Croats (like Serbs) had important foreign friends to assist them in empire-wrecking. Nor that middle-of-the-road, even pacifistic, reformers were lacking. But as time went on, the Croats again began to dream of an independent and separate estate. They expressed dislike of a "Yugoslavia" uniting various (albeit Slavic) nationalities. In their view, no new political unit could counterpoise Austria-Hungary. Furthermore, any conglomeration of Croats and Serbs which the latter would soon control (thought the Croats) was dubious. Union was only pan-Serbism in disguise. Yet another ingredient in Croatian thinking was anti-German sentiment. After Bismarck's fall from favor in 1890, Germany tended to act in concert with her ally Austria and to support exploitation of the Balkans.

I *Zagreb as a Symbol to Matoš*

When the Matoš family moved to Zagreb in 1875, Marija Schams Matoš held strong opinions about where to live. Her husband August's family were plain folk, originally from Hercegovina; he now would teach music in a high school and serve as organist at St. Mark's. But the Schamses (of Dutch descent) enjoyed aristocratic ties and sought to live up to their pretentions. Marija's hopes were directed toward Grič. Stories by her son mention residences with large portals, church roofs varicolored like Easter eggs, impressive clocktowers.[5]

There were two Zagrebs. The Upper City (Gornji Grad, also known as Grič) was old, patrician, historically rich; the Lower City, newer, was less pretentious, an industrial slumland. In a piece entitled "Zagrebački Baedeker" ("A Zagreb Guidebook," 1911) for *Hrvatska sloboda*, Matoš pretends to be a villager touring around in the company of a native guide.[6] The visitor goggles at a Lower-City leather factory, at a statue of *Ban* Jelačić sitting ahorse, his saber pointed toward a tannery. Everywhere there are foreigners: Magyars, Serbs, and Jews. In the Upper City, the streets carry Serbian names, the justice system is Magyarized. Institutions churn out paperwork; a military presence is detectable. Amid it all, to be Croatian is to exist at the lowest level! "Zagreb is nice only for dead people," the native remarks.[7]

Did Matoš grasp too late what was occurring there? The question is asked and affirmatively answered by Marijan Matković, a reputable critic.[8] Matoš certainly loved his city, but he had left it (at age twenty-one) for fourteen years. He carried away a very personal image and when he returned, found it false. Zagreb, for many people, had become the economically important Lower City.

The people, too, had changed. Those who greeted him were not those he remembered. On his Zagreb tour, the stranger sees a sign and asks, "who is John the Baptist Tkalčić?" That is the name of a jolly bartender, he is told, who sings at work like a canary. The Tkalčić family was, in fact, Old Zagreb to the bone; but becoming tainted by white-collar crime, they had scattered. Young Matoš fancied himself in love with Dragica Tkalčić, to whom he addressed his first sonnet.[9] He was also good friends with her brothers, Ivo, Juro and Vladimir, who shared his musical interests. He seems especially to have enjoyed playing Lord Chesterfield in letters (from Paris) to Vladimir, ten years his junior.[10]

The Mažuranić family, also Old Zagreb, lived near the Matoš home at 10 Jurjevska. Bearded, patriarchal Ivan Mažuranić had been in his youth the author of the famous *Death of Smail-Aga Čengić*, a literary epic in the folk manner dealing with an incident on the border of Montenegro and Hercegovina. That was in 1846. After 1848 an interest in politics led him away from poetry (and literature) and, eventually, to the position of *ban*. Now, in the 1880s, he was a symbol, the most distinguished surviving figure of the Illyrian movement, his very name a household word. Ivana Brlić-Mažuranić, the granddaughter and future author, went to school with young Antun. Except by sight he never knew the old man, yet let him stand for the whole of Croatia's aristocratic past. He kept in touch with Ivana until the end.[11]

If Matoš's Zagreb was mostly figment, certain historical verities remain. Here, about 1847, in the homeland of what is known as the *kaj* dialect, Ljudevit Gaj had accepted a Serbian proposal of far-reaching consequence: there would be a common literary language, but Croats would use the Roman (and Serbs, the Cyrillic) alphabet. Here too, at mid-century, Bishop Josip Juraj Strossmayer had founded the first Yugoslav Academy of Sciences, espousing the cultural symbiosis of Croats and Serbs. Finally, here in the 1870s, the cleric-turned-politician Ante Starčević had organized the *Stranka prava* (Faction of the Right). Nowadays it is officially commonplace to describe the Faction as "democratic", which goes counter to the truth. It was, simply, one quarrelsome splinter among many. Much later, the *Stranka* helped Matoš get back from exile. In this sense, it might be said to aim at what *he* conceived as justice and democracy.

Zagreb meant both Strossmayer and Starčević. Matoš found the cleric saintly but ineffectual, lovable but senescent; and compared him to a fertile, fruitful valley in Slavonia.[12] The politico got full marks for patriotism, energy, and effectiveness, although Matoš discerned, withal, a certain waspishness. As he put it, Starčević's mind was "a plateau swarming with wolves and robbers," all vainly seeking to escape. Nevertheless, he admired him to the last, bestowing epithets like *stekliš* ("partisan" in the best sense) and *domać korennik* ("the houseplant").

II *Young Matoš, 1873–1894*

Antun Gustav Matoš was born in the small town of Tovarnik, which he referred to jokingly as "Donkeyville" (Eselheim), in the district of Srem (northwest of Belgrade) on Friday, 13 June 1873, the second of five children.[13] The family moved to Zagreb when he was two. (Incidentally, he did not adopt the name Gustav until much later in life.) An indifferent student, young Antun got through grade seven of the Zagreb Gymnasium. His studies included French and cello, two valuable investments in the future.

Next he attended veterinary school in Vienna (1891–1892), but music and a busy social life were not conducive to veterinary scholarship and soon he was packed off home. By now liable to army service, he was drafted into the Imperial Cavalry during the fall of 1893 and shipped to back-country Slavonia (a region of Croatia lying north of the Sava toward the Danube). His duty consisted of mucking out stables and currying horses. He loathed every day and after eight months contrived reassignment to a farrier's school in Zagreb, with prospects of further schooling in Vienna.

In August 1894, without a word to his family, Matoš deserted from the army. With a friend he left Zagreb for Serbia in hopes of a literary career.[14] A first story, "The Power of Conscience," had already been published in the August 1892 issue of *Vijenac,* a prestigious Zagreb journal once edited by none other than August Šenoa, Zagreb's brightest literary sun. Another story, "Sonata in D-Major," was imminent. On the way to Belgrade there was a mishap when the two were recognized, picked up by police, and thrown in with gypsies and murderers. Luckily they managed to escape and with only one or two more hitches arrived in Belgrade.

III   *Belgrade, 1894–1897*

Belgrade was no picnic, especially during that severe first winter. Matoš took several jobs (tutor, theater cellist, chamber player) before making a connection with Janko Veselinović (1862–1905), a fixture on the Belgrade scene. Janko (as Matoš always refers to him) accepted the young man as a contributor to the short-lived weekly *Pobratim* and later helped him establish links with publications like *Brankovo kolo* in Sremski Karlovci and *Nada* in Sarajevo, the latter edited by Kosta Hörmann. More immediately, Janko provided food and clothing and spiritual comfort. In an essay on Veselinović which he included in *Vidici i putovi* [Outlooks and High Roads, 1907] Matoš, looking back, wrote that " . . . Janko was often father and mother to me, standing by with advice and help in my most difficult hours."[15]

He has left the description of a typical workday:

Every morning about seven I would check in with Janko, across from the Government Printing Office where he was winding up his duties as proofreader of the in-house *Srpske novine*. The job was a sinecure, and several great poets had preceded him in it. Seeing me afoot, like the well-known French king to the well-known place, Janko liked to observe: "Remember, you Croatian genius! When you bottom on a seat here, you touch where Đura Jakšić and the late Vojislav Ilić used to sit!"[16]

Janko might spend an hour writing in longhand the installment of some new novel. Then coffee and a tot of fermented *boza* as they scanned newspapers and prepared for further work. Lunch with

Janko's brother, a professor of theology. A servant mistakes his name for "Makiš" (which is the name of a river). The writer Milovan Glišić happens by. The group drifts toward Topčider Park, but ends up in the Dardanelles Café, where Janko sings anti-Turkish highwaymen's songs to the accompaniment of a *gusle* (a one-stringed, bowed folk instrument used to accompany epic singing). The Dardanelles was located where the National Museum now stands, and anyone worth knowing in the creative set of Matoš's day was likely to be there—writers, actors, and actresses. Janko, or another of the company, regaled everyone with songs of Robber Vujadin and his sons, or the Pasha's runaway slave, while before a big stove backed by velvet drapery. In a letter of August 1897, Matoš apostrophized the place:

Oh you Dardanelles, "Black Cat" of Belgrade, where I was knighted into the order of critics! How many bittersweet hours did I spend in the shadow of those faded velvet drapes over Turkish coffees! In that little spot behind the Knez Mihajlo monument, many were the genuine, the "misguided" and the "soon-to-be" creative talents I got to know. . . .[17]

Belgrade long behind him, he still recalled the stove which "like a hot sun" warmed the backsides of the not-yet-great.

In an early (March 1896) letter from Belgrade to his sister Danica, Matoš mentions the friendliness of the city and its acceptance of him.[18] Janko had opened avenues toward others who were genuinely famous, such as Stevan Sremac, Branislav Nušić, Jovan Ilić, Milovan Glišić, and Radoje Domanović. But the friendships, particularly that with Janko, failed to survive the reviews of *Hajduk Stanko* [Stanko the Highwayman, 1896], Veselinović's major work, a novel which was set in the stirring times of the first Serbian revolt led by Karađorđe. One review appeared in *Brankovo kolo* (April 1897), another in the May issue of *Vijenac*.[19] The tone was, to use his own word, "negative."[20]

Janko's novel is dismissed as both ignorant and inept, an "improvization" scant on believable dialogue and feeling for the period; the author's special gift for recreating village life may have petered out. Obviously, Janko had sought grand effects, in the manner of Victor Hugo, but had failed out of ignorance, for, apparently, he could read Hugo only in translation. Serbs like Janko simply could not match Croats like August Šenoa, when it came to historical fiction.

Many persons already harbored grudges against Matoš for his hostility to the poet Vojislav Ilić (1862–1894). The attack on Janko struck them as ungrateful. And, as the contemporary Serbian critic Velibor Gligorić scarcely needs to add, the heavy-handed Croatian bias won no points.[21] As for Veselinović, he remained alienated from his erstwhile friend and colleague for seven years, making up only just before he died.

Matoš had reason to feel boycotted. Doors were slammed in his face. He lost his musical employment; was labeled a spy; and soon wanted nothing so much as to leave, especially with the onset of winter. Unfortunately, he could not afford to go until, in the nick of time, Kosta Hörmann and others came through with stake money.

He departed in early January 1898. From Munich, in a month's end letter to the readership of *Nada* (in Sarajevo), he bade farewell to Belgrade's food and drink, bedbugs, nameless critics, and "black memories."[22]

IV *Munich and Geneva, 1898–1899*

Matoš had gone to Munich and hoped to stay there. It was cheaper than Belgrade, with lots of beer, pretty waitresses, music, art, and architecture. But learning that deserters like himself could be extradited, he continued to Switzerland. On the train to Geneva he was taken for an anarchist, much to his amusement. This was the time of the Spanish-American War and of the assassination of the Empress Elizabeth, Franz Joseph's wandering, unhappy wife. The Italian anarchist Lucchese stabbed her almost as Matoš arrived in the city.

To live, Matoš had to write. Fortunately, many interesting people—Rousseau, Mme. de Staël, Gibbon, the Polish poet Mickiewicz—were associated with Geneva. He did not lack material. But he needed to catch up on his reading and to do some research: there were serious deficiencies in his education. And there was the matter of literary format. His genre became the "letter from abroad," a composite essay and travel diary. His first letter (8 April 1898) describes Voltaire at Ferney. Another deals with the Villa Deodatti and its sometime occupant George Lord Byron. It was in Switzerland, too, that Matoš (in 1899) wrote an important essay on Stendhal.[23]

The letters had their personal side as well, telling for example of the conclusion of "a Franco-Croatian alliance" with lovely young Jeanette, whom the aspiring author has met on a park bench near a library. Or again, that he lives in a pension whose landlady charges him only sixty francs a month, but that to make up for it she slices the bread "as thin as sausage" and strictly limits the wine.

Poor and hungry, Matoš sought out fellow Yugoslavs in his quest for something to write about. But he was not long for Geneva.

V *Paris, 1899–1904*

Through Kosta Hörmann, Matoš received an invitation to Paris and a plummy job which guaranteed several months of steady income. He arrived in August 1899 to be secretary of the Bosnian Pavilion, a virtual sinecure. It was just about the time of Dreyfus's second trial at Rennes, a continuation of the biggest "event" of the 1890s. After the first trial, Emile Zola became embroiled in the case and had to flee. All France was divided about questions of guilt or innocence, militarism, anti-Semitism, and espionage. Dreyfus was again convicted, then pardoned without restoration (until 1906) of his civil rights.[24]

The Paris Exposition ran from April to October 1900, opening with a 101-gun salute on the thirteenth. Matoš covered it in twenty-six reports to *Hrvatsko pravo* (in Zagreb) under the alternative titles "Impressions" or "Letters from Paris." These were gathered into book form as *Dojmovi* [Impressions] in 1938, twenty-four years after his death. A few of them did appear earlier in *Ogledi* [Perspectives, 1905], a collection of articles; Matoš liked literary mileage where he could get it. The most interesting parts concern fashion, flirtation, a mass at Notre Dame, a visit to the grave of Heine ("the last troubadour"), the plays of Henri Becque, the music of Grieg. Otherwise, they are a chatty but ordinary chronicle of events, exhibits, and people.

Iverje (Chips, 1899), his first collection of stories, all written since 1892, appeared before Matoš left Geneva. Included were "Fresh Cracknels!" and "Mouse," both of which demonstrate a gain in his storytelling stature; the one is a tale of love and adventure, the other deals with the power of dreams. Both were thematically prophetic. (Here and throughout English titles are used in my own translation. Readers interested in original versions may consult the bibliography.)

A second collection, *Novo iverje* [Fresh Chips], followed in 1900. Mostly reprints, it did contain "A Time to Remember," a charming and wholly new evocation of the writer's youthful visits to a farm near Zagreb which belonged to relatives. This rural love story remains among his finest achievements. (See the translation in the appendix.) Portions of the final and much later *Umorne priče* [Tales from Weariness, 1909] also go back to the Paris years, when stories like "The Balcony," "The Sparrow," "The Great Man," and "The Parrot," were written,[25] as were the noncollected "After a New God" and "First Song."[26] The latter, in fact, concludes in the Luxembourg Gardens, as the hero laments his exile and the loss of his sweetheart.

Matoš also wrote criticisms and necrologies. Among his subjects were the Serbian storyteller Laza K. Lazarevič, the poets Jovan Dučić and Milan Rakić; Oscar Wilde, Emile Zola, and Jovan Ilić, a Belgrade orientalist and poet. In his obituary piece on Ilić, the occupant of the hospitable, arabesqued "little yellow house in Palilula" (a section of Belgrade), Matoš reminisced lavishly. He recalled the welcome given to young literary comers-on like himself; how four sons played around the old man as around a mighty oak tree in the yard. He summoned up companionate hours with Janko and Ilić and Sremac back at the Dardanelles; in those days, Ilić liked to call him *Krobota* ("Mr. Croatia").[27] Matoš usually portrayed people as taking kindly to his talent, his personality, or his foibles. That never prevented his repaying them in quite different coin—witness the case of Janko.

Among his new enthusiasms were Maurice Barrès (1862–1923) and Charles Baudelaire. From them, along with Stendhal, he would forge an artistic credo which emphasized distinctiveness, selectivity, and *élitisme*. Barrès, in the words of Larousse, successively cultivated Self, Earth and the Dead, and [finally] Nationalism. The author of *The Garden of Berenice* (1891), *Blood, Pleasure and Death* (1894), and *The Uprooted* (1897), sought to make Frenchmen forget the recent Franco-Prussian War by reorienting them southward toward a Latinate cultural tradition. He made much of words like "Will," "Energy," and "Individualism."

Matoš's essay on Baudelaire was completed in November 1903, but it caused multiple difficulties before he got it published in *Jadran*, a new Trieste journal edited by Ante Tresić-Pavičić, and eventually in his own *Vidici i putovi* [Outlooks and High Roads, 1907], a collection of essays.[28] While not original, the "Baudelaire" sums up Matoš's conception of what underlay images like the flirt and the dandy. The great French poet, no doubt, seemed *sui generis* in those years, and his urban quality probably doubled his appeal to a man like Matoš.

Matoš had begun to keep notebooks in 1895. In Paris, he filled six more with quotations, usable phrases, and chronological notes. They were his closest approach to a diary. Davor Kapetanić has shown how fruitfully Matoš exploited his stores.[29] Many items found their way into stories, articles, and essays. Among the jottings for 1900: he wanted a list of Jewish names. Could *Dučić* (the poet's name) be derived from Latin *dux* ("leader"), thereby suggesting aristocratic origins? Where to use the Hobbesian *Croatia Croatae lupus* ("Croatia is a wolf to Croats")? He identified himself with his homeland. The notebooks contain effusions like "I stand for [all] Croats who are tormented and harrassed"; or "being Croatian is the only thing about which I am sincere."[30]

He spent much time on correspondence.[31] Matoš was forever embroiled over articles and his need for money. He dispatched hundreds of letters to editors, such as Kosta Hörmann *(Nada)*, Janko Ibler *(Narodne novine)*, Branko Vodnik *(Mlada hrvatska* and *Savremenik)*.[32] Other letters went to members of the family; to friends, like Vladimir Tkalčić; to writers, like Milivoj Dežman, Andrija Milčinović. Matoš kept moving around, and many of his letters may have been lost.

His financial situation was nothing but precarious. As an alien, Matoš could not get steady employment. He wrote; traded rare books; made money in any way which came to mind. He lived in rented rooms and cheap hotels, often writing in bed because of the cold, frequently leaving in the middle of the night for lack of money to settle a bill.

Though scarcely affordable, Matoš's Paris was an exciting place; it was the City of Light. There was an abundance of music (Debussy, D'Indy), poetry (Hérédia, Leconte de Lisle) and literature (Daudet, Anatole France), not to speak of art. Yvonne Guilbert and Cleo de Mérode were stellar attractions. If the parks were, in Hausmann's words, "the lungs of Paris," the boulevards, too, teemed with color and life; they were the domain of toughs in red belts and long shawls, "Apache Indians," who set upon pedestrians, choking and robbing them.

Some problems diminished after acquaintance with the artist André Rouveyre, who did a portrait depicting Matoš as "an exuberant bull." Rouveyre gave him a room (Hotel Cronstadt, rue Jacob); passed along a mistress, Jeanne; even introduced him to friends, such as the anarchist intellectual Meczyslaw Goldberg (1870–1907), the minor Polish poet Wincenty Korab Brzozowski (Vincent de Korab, 1877–1941), and the bookseller Edouard Champion.

How Matoš viewed the Parisian scene depended upon his circum-

stances or upon his correspondent. In a letter (8 December 1901) to
Andrija Milčinović, he sits in the catbird seat and chronicles a typical
day:

> How do I live? I sleep from 3:00–4:00 P.M. Then to a café, where I meet
> my Poles: Bohemians, journalists, working people, revolutionaries. Poles are
> the only Slavs I like. Today we were supposed to burn the Prussian colors and
> an effigy of Wilhelm II in front of the German consulate, but we were too
> few.
> In the evening, if I don't have money, I stay home in the hotel. A pretty
> young neighbor entertains me, singing and fussing with her baby. If flush, I
> go to a girly café and crawl through Paris till dawn. Then, tired and
> exhausted and suffering the pangs of the evening, I lie awake and ask myself:
> how much longer?[33]

Yet in a more sober letter (10 September 1902) to his father, he
describes Paris life as miserable and demoralizing and, all in all,
"rather monotonous."

VI   *Belgrade Again, 1904–1908*

Matoš regarded Belgrade as a way-station to Zagreb. Like the hero
of the story "First Song," he had become disenchanted with foreign
residence; had become, in his own words, a *bijela vrana* ("white
raven"). He wanted to be closer to Olga Herak (1884–1963), a schoolmate with whom he had reestablished contact; years later, she was to
become his fiancée. Also, Belgrade would put him in a more com-
manding position with respect to the *Hrvatska moderna* ("Croatia
Today"), a group of young writers in search of a leader.

Zagreb remained out of season, except for furtive trips (which he
initiated in 1905). The law of the lion awaited deserters there. But Belgrade did not mean the law of the lamb. Quite the contrary. Alexander
Obrenović and his queen were assassinated in June 1903, and under
the new regime Serbia began to withdraw from the Austrian orbit;
Matoš's Croatian sympathies were all the less welcome in that context.
Also unwelcome was his friendship with Kosta Hörmann in Sarajevo,
for Bosnia-Hercegovina had been occupied by Austria since the Congress of Berlin. Its formal annexation in 1908 was marked by a huge
outcry in Belgrade and by deepening resentment throughout Serbia.
Yet, in one sense, the annexation was a necessity to Matoš: no amnesty,

no return home. Above all, over his years abroad he had remained *persona non grata* in Belgrade literary circles. Ironically, his own description of (Paris) bohemians as "more harmful than useful," in a 1904 issue of *Slobodna reč*, happened to express the sentiments of the Belgrade professor and critic Jovan Skerlić (1877–1914), whose stomach churned at the very mention of words like *habitué* and Skadarlija Café (the Dardanelles had been demolished in 1902).[34] Skerlić was a socialist; he appreciated common sense, sincerity, moral values in literature; and he was an unreconstructed Serbophile.

Inevitably, he and Matoš locked horns, which was not surprising in view of their many temperamental and philosophical differences. The air was soon full of epithets like "hatmaker's son" *(Šeširljić)* or "Swiss Socrates" (Skerlić had taken a doctorate in literature at Lausanne). Regrettably, it was a strained time in the lives of both men. Matoš, on his financial uppers, faced the difficulties of resettling in Belgrade. Skerlić confronted a multitude of crises arising from the death in quick succession of his father, elder sister, and a child, not to mention the passing of several friends. Matoš's personal attacks hurt deeply. (See also chapter 3 below.)

Mortality had thinned the ranks of former cronies. To be sure, Matoš met new friends like Borisav Stanković, the playwright and novelist. But many of the old crowd were either already dead or imminently to die. He would soon turn out obituaries for Bishop Strossmayer and Janko (1905) and Stevan Sremac (1906), to name three.[35] It was all depressing, like the Belgrade housing situation. A letter of 1907 describes the rooms as cold, damp, and smelly.[36]

He plunged into drama criticsm, writing for *Samouprava*, employing pseudonyms like Hop-Frog, Gilles, or simply "M." A few stories appeared: "Pretty Helen" in *Hrvatsko pravo*, "A Ministerial Paté" in *Prosveta*, "Solo Variations" in *Savremenik*, all during 1906. And he began to write poetry, attributing this new endeavor to "writer's cramp."[37]

More and more, he turned to the essay form, whether for an obituary, review, or occasional piece. Minor efforts treat "the Barrèsian cult of energy;" Yugoslav noses; professors as a characterless caste—these submitted to *Slobodna reč*;[38] Ralph Waldo Emerson (1904) and Guy de Maupassant (1907).[39] His best work was gathered into *Vidici i putovi* (*Look-Outs and High Roads*, 1907): "Bishop Strossmayer's Memorial" and "Baudelaire," for example.[40]

VII Zagreb, 1908–1914

After obtaining amnesty in January 1908, Matoš finally left Serbia. Once back in Zagreb, he ingratiated himself with a group known as Frankists. Dr. Josip Frank had assumed leadership of the right upon the death of Ante Starčević. He bore a non-Croatian name and is usually characterized as amenable to demands from Vienna. Matoš acknowledged all that, but believed that Frank possessed a "strong Croatian heart.' The new allegiance did not last for long. Matoš began to fight with his former friends.

Misgauging Zagreb as he had earlier misgauged Belgrade, Matoš found himself no longer at home there, socially or politically. Neither the powerful new bourgeois of the Lower City nor the impoverished aristocrats of Grič looked kindly upon nonconformists, to say nothing of erstwhile deserters. He experienced hostility. Far from floating into the literary scene and imposing his intelligence on the elements, he felt shunned by the Establishment. And when he launched several journals (one with the name Kokot ["Cock"]) aiming at literary excellence, all failed. Financial problems grew worse. He was reduced to taking an examination qualifying him as a high-school teacher of French. That became his source of livelihood.

Matoš's coterie included the young and Whitmanesque poet Tin Ujević (1891–1955), whose extended later sojourns in Paris, Belgrade, Sarajevo, and Split, winding up in Zagreb, rivaled those of the rabbi, as Matoš was now being called. But soon the rabbi became embroiled with just about everyone, Ujević included. It was usual for him to charge plagiarism, often on the most trivial grounds. What distinguished the confrontation with Ujević was being taxed himself with stealing from Maurice Barrès![41] Yet he was in his element and he proceeded with zest. As if he relished being under attack, he included anti-Matoš material with his own polemics, epigrams, and satires—a fact which, as the most recent editor observes, makes Dragi naši savremenici [Our Dear Contemporaries, 1912] unique in Yugoslav literature.[42] He attacked Savremenik, the organ of the Association of Croatian authors, because he did not like what they published—altogether a curious circumstance, considering that he himself served on the editorial board. He charged Pokret, a progressivist journal, with being pro-Serbian because it espoused ideas of the Czech scholar T. G. Masaryk (1850–1937), later to become that country's first president. The name *Pokret* ("The Movement"), he transposed to *Pokržet*, suggesting a foreign origin, and he referred to its staff as *pokreteni*, a word play intended to make one think of "cretins."

The best works of this period are poems, criticisms, and travel pieces. True, a final story collection *Umorne priče* [Tales from Weariness] appeared in 1901; but it does not match what preceded. A few uncollected stories are of interest because of unusual (not to say forbidden!) themes. "Lila" deals with homosexuality. "Everything Happens," with gang-rape and acid-splashing. "A Common Story," with emancipated women and venereal disease.[43]

Matoš the poet reached his stride after 1909. A succession of good poems, mostly in sonnet form, include "Morning Rain," "Archilochus," "A Dialogue in Grič," "Autumn Evening," and "Nocturne." These and other poems are the subject of chapter 4 below.

Again, the volume *Naši ljudi i krajevi* [Our People at Home, 1910] contains good critical essays, such as "Books and Authors" or "Modernism." In his last years, Matoš was increasingly concerned with style, which he equated with individuality. Style came first and was to be valued even above sensibility.[44] He quarreled with the socially minded ("synthetic") Zagreb critic Milan Marjanović about tendentiousness in art. Art, according to Matoš, need *not* be moral, practical, social, or political. Their dispute focused in the end on stylistics. As he says, devastatingly, Marjanović simply did not know style.[45]

Matoš denounced fads. True modernism, he would assert, transcends novelty by being a way in which modern civilized man looks at the world. Well aware of trends, he perceived a drift from romanticism.[46] At the same time, he wrote sympathetically about romantic poets, such as Jovan Dučić or Milan Rakić; Jean Jacques Rousseau or the Croatian poet Kranjčević.[47] Matoš had certain prejudices regarding the plastic arts. His criticism of Ivan Meštrović's sculpture as being "un-Croatian" is controversial, to say the least.[48] On the other hand, his essay "The Painter Menci Klement Crnčić" (1910) is both sensitive and well-informed.[49] Crnčić (1865–1930) did impressionistic Croatian landscapes.

After 1908, the work is more and more Croatia-oriented. He travels, for example, to historical sites like Lobor, Križevac, Samobor, the coastal region.[50] In "A Field of Nobility" (1913), he revisits "the cannon of Turopolje" in country associated with the historical novels of August Šenoa. Of course, he contributed to *Obzor* other lighter-hearted material: he attended a convention of gypsies, he observed swimmers and sunbathers along the Sava. But in general, his interest exceeded the merely curious or touristic.

Matoš sought to relate landscape and people; to explain the *Croatian soul* by geography in the same way that Maurice Barrès (and, before him, Hippolyte Taine) had attempted to explain the French soul. His basic idea is that landscape can be used to evoke history. Lobor brings to mind the ancient Keglević barons, whose seat it was. Samobor evokes Stanko Vraz, a nineteenth-century romantic poet. Vraz may have been an adoptive Croat, but he glorified Croatia's flora and fauna. Matoš would like nothing better than to summon up the dead poet from these ashes. "Travel is the poetry of modern civilization," he had remarked in his early essay "Holidays" (1902).

It is as if, by extolling Vraz, he were dipping into an inexhaustible reservoir of folk energy and ladling out an elixir which would refresh Croatia and inspire her anew. The process had distinctly nationalistic and racial overtones—as Barrès flatly conceded in France. Matoš must have realized all that; but he feigned innocence. And if he *did* take a page from Barrès's book, he used those ideas without attribution.[51] Until his erstwhile disciple, Ujević, caught him out.

It is not so clear that Matoš cared about Barrès at the end. Ill with throat cancer—an affliction to which the entire family was susceptible—he sought medical treatment and a change of scene in Italy, visiting first Florence (1911), then Rome (1913). The journeys appear among his travel pieces. If the precious and affected style was intended to evoke Barrès's lyricism, it more readily brings to mind the babblings of a travel writer like Myra Waldo. The inspiration simply is not there. A single exception to that harsh judgment is "Roman Outings," where he evokes Pamfili, Nemi, and Tivoli.[52] His schoolboy memories of the poet Horace return in a rush.

Pečalba (Day Labor, 1913), a medley of work published between 1902 and 1912, was his final collection. The profiles include P. T. Barnum, Isadora Duncan, Ignace Paderewski, and Count Tolstoy. Of more interest are reminiscences of Paris and Zagreb and of his escape to Belgrade. But it is really ephemera, as he himself allows.

He never married Olga Herak, giving the excuse that if married she would lose her teaching job. She took a husband after his death and eventually emigrated to Argentina. He died, in hospital, on 17 March 1914. His last words ("I have burned out!") were bitter; the sense is of a guttering candle. He was buried in Mirogoj Cemetery, to be followed six months later in death by August Matoš, his father.

VIII   *Approaches to Matoš*

Using Matoš to explain Matoš can only thwart the critic or baffle the reader. He was supremely inconsistent: "I like fat women . . ." "I don't like fat books or fat women."[53] More substantial contradictions go to the man's image: how did he think about himself? How did others perceive him? He acknowledged the contrariety. "Perhaps no emerging artist is evaluated so variously," he writes in a 1901 letter from Paris.[54] To some he appears tragic; to others comic. People question his objectivity, his very sincerity. Some see in him a hack; others, a hero.

Any self-respecting critic who expands upon Matoš's self-judgments must proceed with caution. Even his Zagreb varied. Now he sees Grič, now the Lower City; now, Germans or Hungarians, now Croats; now, contemporary Zagreb, now the abode of the folk hero Petrica Kerempuh or the sixteenth-century execution site of the peasant revolutionary Matija Gubec.[55]

Similar difficulties arise with his reading. By his own account, Matoš got out of school with Latin and French. (The status of his German is disputable.) In Vienna, according to the claim, he read Kant and Schopenhauer—a path leading to certain despair, he says, had he not been rescued by art. There can be little doubt about his French. His "three B's" were Beyle (Stendhal), Baudelaire, Barrès; he read them deeply, if he ready anyone at all.

But how deeply did he, or could he, read the hundreds of authors mentioned in his work? He knew Edgar Allan Poe in a French translation, probably the vehicle which was most accessible. Even so, much of his vaunted knowledge was in smidgins. There had to be blind spots when it came to English, Spanish, Italian, even German literature. Beyond Europe, whole areas (e.g. Persian or Chinese) were deficient. When Matoš strayed too far afield (as in some of his letters from the Paris Exposition), the results were embarrassing. Characteristically, however, not embarrassing to him.

Where can an honest account be found? If a man attitudinizes even in his notebooks and correspondence, where does he reveal what really makes him tick? In the end, Matoš's words have no meaning, except in relation to certain basic facts, the two most significant of which are that he *had to survive;* and that he managed to be interesting. Anything else—that he was a dreamer, a stylist, a humorist, a Croat; that he read and accumulated broadly, despite deficiencies in background and training; that, in constant financial straits, he wheedled and nagged: all that is secondary. "I have survived and did not expect to do so," he says at one point. As he aged, he felt driven and became yet more ill-tempered and sarcastic. Everything had to be done immediately. It was not as if he could wait.

His illusions extend beyond Zagreb. Recurrently he wanted to emi-grate to America, the land of dreams, where he would be a journalist. He portrays himself as a personality to whom others readily take or attach themselves. Yet he delights in being divided; he talks with his shadow, plays a repertory of character roles—Don Juan; clown; Croa-tian patriot; Bohemian; Diogenes. In his reviews he includes questions to which he does not expect an answer; foreign-language quotations which (since he himself transcribed them incorrectly in the notebooks) would not be understood.

He must have attention; how he got it was immaterial. Nor did sin-cerity come into view. Fortunately, most readers occasionally got a flash and recognized in him, as it were, an old friend or congenial spirit. Humor was his great device—the light boyish whimsy, rather than the heavy brute sarcasm of later years which he thought would convey the weight of authority. His presentation is brilliant. Obviously, he loves language; spends much time devising anagrams, puns, ripostes. At worst, he is the caricaturist, distorter, and twister.

He forever preached style. Poetry meant the sonnet, and he had his own ideas about sonnet form. The first two stanzas ought to be iden-tical, he informs the poet Milan Rakić in a criticism.[56] But he felt no constraint to follow the advice himself.

No one did more to blur genres or confound travelogues, criticisms, fantasies, and essays. The journalist's eye and nose and ear were in superb working order when it came to color, texture, earth and sky. He is fascinated by noses; bird songs; details such as the location of toilets in provincial Šokac churches. He has a knack for manipulating details, balancing one against another. The seesaw effect can disquiet a reader.

Matoš is mastered by powerful enthusiasms (Barrès, Baudelaire) and equally powerful antipathies (Tolstoy, Zola). His work shows pervers-ities of preference: French music exists, German music does not. He is more propagandist than critic. Certainly, his chauvinism and *macho* stance (on issues like women's rights) appear dreadfully old-fashioned today.

"My Bacchus is mainly Croatian."[57] Some would say that, without Croatia, he is unimaginable. A defender of the autonomy of art, he also penned the essay "Art and Nationalism" (1912), where he maintains that "patriotism is our first and most sacred obligation."[58] According to Matoš, all art is national and patriotic, though the artist himself need not be a patriot (and though patriotism by itself is not art). Nonnational art is the mere raw imitation of some foreign model. But while large cultural entities like France and England can wear motley, the problem of a small country like Croatia is quite different. Croatia must retain linguistic and stylistic purity, unless she is to be Germanized or Magyarized. In Croatia, patriotism, at least in the language context, is thus a condition of artistic survival.

Above all, Matoš cuts an interesting figure. "Everything fascinated me." That is how Ivo Andrić in his commemorative remarks epitomizes the man: he wanted to see, feel, smell, hear everything; to pick up every nuance; to experience it all, to talk, to react. In Andrić's words:

He loved life, art. Partial to personal courage, he admired all values, old or new; sinful and sick he might be, but never middle-class. Perhaps best, he was the sworn enemy of Mr. Stupid and Mr. Commonplace, hated their "swamp world" and their unshakeable composure. He was always visible, never passive or neutral; always the activist, *engagé* one way or the other.[59]

To be Matoš, said Andrić, meant never to be tedious.

CHAPTER 2

The Storyteller

MATOŠ remained a storyteller to the end. "The Power of Conscience," first of sixty stories, was published in 1892. "For the People," the last, seems to have been written in 1913, one year before he died. Although he was paid for it (as he would say, "got an honorarium"), the piece did not appear until 1924.

With rare exceptions, he published in periodicals, then gathered about half of the stories into three collections: *Iverje* [Chips, 1899]; *Novo iverje* [Fresh Chips, 1900]; and *Umorne priče* [Tales from Weariness, 1909].[1] He had a hard time finding financial backers. The influential publishing house, Matica hrvatska, did not acknowledge his need until the very last, granting a loan only when he was far gone with cancer. His correspondence was extensive; how many stories were lost, whether by editors or in transit, will never be known.[2] Finally, tales outside the collections have now been brought together in volume 2 of the *Sabrana djela (Collected Works)* by Matoš's latest editor, Dragutin Tadijanović. They vary in quality, but a good half dozen rival those chosen by the author himself.

In what follows, Matoš's stories are given English titles. For readers interested in Serbo-Croatian, the orginals appear in the bibliography.

I Iverje

The stories in *Iverje* [Chips, 1899] were published between 1892 and 1899: "The Power of Conscience" (1892), "Ingratitude" (1897), "The Welcoming Speech" (1896), "Fresh Cracknels!" (1897), "Statue of the Motherland, Summer 188—" (1895), and "Mouse" (1899). As is evident, there was no concern about arranging them chronologically. "Fresh Cracknels!" and "Mouse" are probably the best known. The others may seem rather crude today; but certain details, such as the soirée setting of "Ingratitude," are of interest in relation to later work.[3]

Matoš's first story takes the form of a dream fantasy. Joso Cicvarić, a bibulous clerk, accepts walking sticks as bribes from peasants, but does not process their petitions. One night he dreams that the sticks come to life and drive him, first, to a neighbor's house, to a brook, to the moon, and finally back to earth in a fiery fall. Jolted awake, he decides to limit his wine consumption.

Most stories use the traditional third-person narrator. In *this* one, when Joso crashes and is sniffed by an old dog named Bundaš (who detects burned flesh in the "fallen meteorite"), he is aware both of being sniffed and of observing the action. The author, too, has a double vision. After an impersonal beginning he invites the reader to share confidences about "our" scribe or "poor" Cicvarić. Yet Matoš ends as he began, distancing himself from his materials. For all its plain start and finish, the tale generally tends toward the mock heroic. In flight from the sticks, Joso "takes off through the window like a quail," they pursuing him "like a swarm of winged snakes." At the brook, his pockets are filled with frogs; the nose of this keen-scented clerk from the Lika drips with catarrh.

"The Power of Conscience" has affinities with "Among Strangers" and "A Christmas Story" in *Novo iverje*; with "Path to Nowhere" and "Autumn Idyll" in *Umorne priče;* and with Matoš's final "For the People." All deal with dreams, derangements, fantasies. (See the following section.)

If not dreams, the theme may be love. "Fresh Cracknels!" is one of many tales with a heroine. Penniless Dragica and her widowed mother move from Zagreb to Lipovac (in Slavonia), where she runs the postal telegraph office. A lonely life, not made easier by certain inhabitants of the place. Still, her beauty attracts two suitors: a recruit named Ivan Unukić (the hero) and Franz Kurt Maria Joseph Hans Wurstler von Wurstlingen (the villain), a hussar commandant and relentless womanizer. Unukič breaks in a fine English stallion which Wurstler has won at cards; but when his riding antics cause alarm, Wurstler strings him up as punishment. Dragica, at last in love, cuts him down. Happily, they marry and raise a family, while Wurstler's numerous cruelties bring his dismissal from the army and his decline, first to waiter, then to vendor of pork cracknels. This story, too, does not stand alone. Almost every year Matoš thought up a new variation on the theme of love.

A third motif in *Iverje* is death. "Statue of the Motherland," "The Welcoming Speech," and "Mouse" are all stories about that—three out of the six. In Matoš, death is always near at hand and multifarious. It may be the result of a bet, a practical joke; rejection or starvation; trampling, slashing, drowning, syphilitic complications, war. In the first tale, an elderly fruit vendor and his wife die when the government summons mounted troops to quell a demonstration in Zagreb. The old woman is in no way connected with the events and simply does not want to leave Jelavić Square; but she gets trampled by a hussar patrol. The grieving husband drinks himself to death. Both are buried secretly. "Welcoming Speech" refers to a metrical greeting in which young Ljubica has been coached by her guardian. She delivers it in honor of newly arrived Count X. Ljubica is a sensitive but unbalanced girl, whose mother had worked for the count's predecessor. When he drunkenly kisses her she is revulsed, runs away, and freezes to death. A friendly, would-be rescuer also dies.

Finally, "Mouse" is a nickname shared by another Ljubica (Ljubica Kolarička) and her lover Mihajlo Milinović, an egotistical medical student who has made her pregnant. She lives in the household of Mihajlo's uncle, where nothing is known of her condition; he lives in the city. Mihajlo does not want to marry until he is out of school. In letters, he urges an abortion—so insistently and abusively, in fact, that Ljubica commits suicide. After a bad night, dreaming about mice with enormous tails and steely teeth who want to devour him, he records his impressions, as always, in a diary. Meanwhile, he has been playing with a revolver and, inadvertently, has left a string tied to the trigger. A mouse gnaws at the string, the gun goes off, and Mihajlo is killed.

Some further stories standing in the tradition of "Mouse" are discussed below.

II Novo iverje

Matoš's second collection, Novo iverje [Fresh Chips, 1900], contains stories written between 1898 and 1900: "A Time to Remember" (1900), "Among Strangers" (1898), "The Parrot" (1900), and "Lonely Night" (1900). That these were years of foreign residence may account both for the occasional sharp nostalgia (as in "A Time to Remember") and for the general cosmopolitan milieu. Like its predecessor, Novo iverje deals with love, death, dreams, although these elements may be mixed in the same story as in "The Parrot," an account of adulterous love and death and dreams.

By and large, the stories can be paired. "Lonely Night" and "A

Needle-like Man" focus on death. In the first, the narrator makes a fanciful and fatal visit, in the company of Charon, to the City of Death. Spent candle smoke and burned incense fill his nostrils. Some dead monks are discovered; lying on the steps of a church, they resemble black notes in a medieval missal. The narrator expires in the cemetery as he is attempting to record his final impressions. The text breaks off. It bears some likeness, formally, to a poem in prose.

In the second, the hero (a man of peculiar physiognomy and temperament) cannot hold on to anything, occupationally or intellectually, until he makes a trip to Slavonia. There he meets a young girl, to whom he proposes. But before they can be wed, he fatally stabs himself with her hatpin.

Again, "Among Strangers" and "A Christmas Story" both deal with dreams and madness. A fugitive anarchist has fallen into the hands of a sadistic count and his Chinese servant who ply him with champagne, hoping to use him in unspeakable experiments. Through a drunken haze the anarchist becomes aware of his plight. He dreams of a cat being chased by dogs; of two blind peasants fighting one another, who break off and suddenly turn on him. Although just managing to evade the count's knife and to make his escape, he loses his sanity.

The hero of "A Christmas Story" is already mad. Unemployed and close to starvation, living in Munich, he writes letters to an erstwhile fiancée who has, in fact, rejected him. They stand little chance of delivery, in any event, for they bear the address of a brewery. Preoccupied with thoughts of death, yet weary to his very bones, hardly does the wretched man finally doze off when the clock strikes seven and awakes him. He hears his neighbors' holiday merriment; thinks of his widowed mother who keeps house for a priest; tries to capture and devour a stray puppy. Meanwhile, second-tier comments are provided by a diaristic bulldog named Flock, who regards his master as lion-hearted if plainly stupid. Flock eventually locates and brings home the mother and fiancée, but by now the hero has fallen silent forever. "Never more was there a word from him," the story concludes. In short, he died.

Incongruity is sometimes the cue to an alternative perception of reality. Startled, the moviegoer sees wash flapping on a clothesline, a sequence apparently unrelated to the plot; or watches someone walking down a corridor. It is a moment out of a stranger's story. In *8½*, Fellini evokes a different movement of time, another reality, by effects of lighting or by picture composition.[4] With Matoš, it is some unusual,

jarring detail like the mal-addressed letters or the blindness of the shepherds. Indeed, such hints not infrequently occur in dreams. In a late
story of 1913 called "The Stovepipe Hat," the protagonist, obsessed
with his headpiece, wears it constantly. Once he dreamed that a stork
carried a similar hat, that the hat contained a child, and that the child
was—himself! Identification with the hat is so strong that when his
lady friend spills coffee on it, their romance abruptly ends. Again, the
hero of the posthumously published "For the People," a teacher who
has refused to back a certain political candidate, is in real danger of
losing his job. In low spirits, he dreams about his family and sees before
him a door pierced by a black hole. Inserting his hand, he feels teeth
and at the same time hears the moan of an infant. A vision ensues of
his baby son, face covered with blood, in rags, sitting on a chair. Is
there not something incongruous in this association of infancy with
teeth, blood, and moans? By the end of the story matters have
improved to the point where it is likely that the candidate will be
defeated. At a preelection mass the hero launches into the Croatian
national anthem and is joined by the congregation. For the man's son,
the singing inspires a vision of St. George with all the other saints in
glory. Saints, on one hand; on the other, mundane political reality. Yet
more incongruity.

Dreams serve a variety of purposes for this author, seemingly. A pre-
monitory dream warns characters who are about to die. The crazed
girl in "Welcoming Speech," from his first collection, hears the voice
of her dead mother, and in "Parrot" Alfred Kamenski's vision of his
late mother presages his own death—this from the second collection,
Novo iverje. Matoš used the device to supply hitherto unknown information. In addition, he saw that it permitted contrary temporal movement: forward or back, within or without. He understood how waking
and dreaming are not simple opposites, knew too that many an eccen-
tricity could occur in dreams. The Marquis de Sade and an Austrian
writer of the nineteenth century, Leopold de Sacher-Masoch, were
familiar to him, although merely because of their odd-ball material.
The age of Freud lay beyond his ken. Nor did he provide the sort of
dream grammar that a Wittengenstein would have wished.[5] Nevertheless, he contrived changes of mode and effectively used dreams in an
updated if still fundamentally romantic way.

The two remaining stories in *Novo iverje*, both from 1900, treat different kinds of love. "Camao," the Serbo-Croatian title of "The Parrot," refers to a mythical medieval bird which dies when a wife betrays

her husband. The plot concerns the adulterous liaison of a pianist (Alfred Kamenski) and a certain Fanny Forest, the latter already married to an American artist. Their romance is betrayed to the husband, first by an old retainer, then by a parrot which repeats their conversation (hence the English title). Enraged, the husband slays everything in sight *except* the bird.

"A Time to Remember" recounts a banishment made happy by passionate youthful love. Because of a schoolboy prank—the attempted inebriation of a neighbor known as "Goatgirl"—the narrator has been packed off to the household of a relative who is the parish priest in nearby Hrastovac (in reality, Brezovica, about two hours from Zagreb). There he meets Smiljka, an unbalanced, short-lived Ophelia. Their affair ends with his departure; when the narrator returns five years later the girl is dead, and many other things have changed. (See the translation of this story in the appendix.) Much attention is given to farm life and to social types like pipe-smoking Uncle Grga, the priest, or hospitable Aunt Tončika (Antonija). The parade of colorful visitors includes a "Turkey Baron," who has lost his wife to a lover; a member of the National Assembly, with actress friend, both driven off by a mischievous bull; an interior decorator (and amiable skirt-chaser) from Spain; a fictional counterpart of the poet August Harambašić (1861–1911); and an anti-Semitic Jew, who enjoys playing at the celebration of mass. The story's construction, as may be guessed, is episodic.

III   *Umorne priče*

After 1902, Matoš moved to a new position with regard to his heroines. The early ones had been fragile creatures, their frequent pallor his Victorian shorthand for gentle birth and moral purity. Intellectual types and bluestockings like George Sand never did fare well at his hands: Matoš favored the girl next door. His were good girls—wholesome, sisterly, sweetheartly; neither introspective, nor overeducated, nor overly concerned with emancipation. Unsanctioned sexual activity was simply beyond their horizon. In the stories later collected as *Umorne priče* [Tales from Weariness, 1909], however, we begin to notice a tougher breed of heroine, by comparison to whom the male protagonist comes off a poor second. An early example is "The Balcony" (1902), a story told in the first person and against himself by a man who abstractly adores Woman, classically mounted as on a pedestal—the balcony of the title—but who feels uncomfortable with her real life flesh and blood counterparts.

The plot runs as follows: Eugene returns after some years to his native city and calls upon his old love Cvijeta, only to discover that her family has fallen on hard times and that she now lives in an isolated, cold, garret flat. He catches her interest and leads her toward thoughts of marriage with his story about falling in love with a balcony. A charming little structure, it was attached to an old, crumbling mansion with aristocratically tall windows, within a secluded park in a distant city. Although the gracefully convex balustrade was covered with moss and creepers which concealed the delay of its marble supports, the balcony yet seemed to Eugene seductive and coquettish, accessible, scaled to human dimensions. All summer long, as he tells the story to Cvijeta, he paid court to it, fastening back its luxuriant, trailing vines revealingly, "like a wedding gown," and climbing up to pillow his head on the swelling breast of his "cold victim."

Indeed, the human analogy is scarcely veiled and recalls Poe's "facial" treatment of the house of Usher: Eugene's abandoned balcony is like a "frozen, rococco smile" against the yellowed, mossy walls of the house, which are "wet with patches of rain, like an old man's tearful face." Again, its delicate, wrought-iron work suggested a fan held by "yellow, worm-eaten hands" and evoked in the beholder a feeling of sadness and anxiety.

In very fact there does materialize here, late one afternoon, one of nature's vestals:

For on my dusk-purple balcony, spent with yearning, was a woman, . . . a woman naked, proud, noble as a goddess, bursting with vigor, luscious as a grape. Her light, gauzy wrap floated off behind her like a cloud. Had she been brought to life by the summer air? Was that a sun's ray infusing her with red, human blood? Could that divine light as it waned have become a woman? She leaned her white, flawless elbows on the rotted handrail of my . . . our balcony. Over her bare, shapely shoulders were strewn heavy tresses, a queenly fleece of yellow gold, and she gazed into the distance with a blue and shining tranquillity, like sky seeking the sun. I vainly tried to stop that sun as it set, digging my fingers into the hungry earth. Through the foliage and drifting light came the voice of an unseen bird at dusk: a tender, saucy, merry, wanton sound, like a fountain turned on only that morning beneath the late moon; the marvellous, oboelike voice became transformed into songs and echoes from the balcony. The last rays of the sun flared, broke and contracted in a spasmodic orgy, spilling down upon the human beauty which was held up to it by my faithful, antique balcony. Finally the weary sun paled to yellow and then to blue as it gathered mansion, ruined garden, and woman into its tired, cold shadows. Yet she, the goddess-spirit of my noble, old balcony, straightened like a slender palm tree, stretched out her white arms to the lofty, ruddy heights in the West as if to a rosy altar. She was reaching sun-wards! Her thighs glowed like two vessels of everlasting red wine, and her breasts gleamed and glistened in the light of evening, they flamed as though containing the torches of new Cains and new Abels, the stars of new heavens. Nothing else could I see, nothing else could I hear, as with her pale, weak arms she stopped the flow of time. . . .[6]

Leaping out from the shrubbery on all fours, the young man bursts into a paean of adoration which is barely launched when he glimpses, half-concealed behind the woman—Mephistopheles! And, to the lugubrious whines and howls of an unseen canine chorus, he watches as she is unceremoniously yanked indoors by an angry fist, yellowed and bony.

Cvijeta ("Blossom") is similarly tall and fair of figure, with full lips and luxuriant, red-gold hair, with fresh violets at her breast, where once she wore Eugene's roses. He observes that her clothes have not changed over the years, also that her slippers are ridiculously down at the heel. Like them, his own feelings now go awry, "shredding and twisting to the left," and he brusquely rejects the girl's advances. Next morning, ashamed, he asks Cvijeta's pardon and, with consummate gall, begs her to write. At the same time he notices how she lets her skirts drag in the roadside mud to hide those heels, embarrassing reminders of decline. Proudly the girl refuses even to look at Eugene, who now trails her like a whipped cur, and her final word is: "Never!"

In the framed story, Eugene's mansion burns down. By his return visit, its lovely park is a barnyard, his beloved balcony a drying rack for underwear atop a farm dungheap. All has yielded in the end to loathsome age, much like Eugene himself. He caricatures himself as an impotent and bloated baboon, a rhinoceros with a toothache. Matoš here intended more than an allegory of decay and death. True, behind the fair, green-wreathed form lurked the grinning skeleton. But what matters are the two heroines and the contrasts between them. In the demonic lady of the balcony, as well as in Cvijeta's "toughness," there is something different.

The new breed of heroine can also be glimpsed in the callous lady of "I Have Killed Her!"—the exclamation of a sculptor who thinks he has lost the pathetic young woman whom he rescued from domestic service. They had become separated. When later he thinks he sees her, in fine fettle, on the arm of a soldier, he is not acknowledged. In consternation, he feels that the original lady is dead and he responible.

Very likely the two women were, after all, one and the same: it is merely a matter of perception. Similarly in "Pretty Helen," where a young painter is much affected when a silken-blonde visits his household. Years later, as an art student in Paris, he spends the night with a masked lady resembling his youthful vision—only to lose her (still unidentified!) by morning. Again, near Avignon he thinks he has found her, now along with a husband. He bursts in and threatens them. But they do not recognize him. He is arrested and sent to prison.

Both types appear in those stories which Matoš did not choose to collect. Danica, in "First Song" (1901), represents tradition. She offers herself in marriage to a willy-nilly journalist with whom she has sung a Schubert duet, only to be refused because he takes rather longer than she to make up his mind. Too late, in exile he rues his loss. Marta Gorska, an actress, is already the mistress of a powerful Hungarian noble ("After a New God," 1902). Her new affair with the indecisive, exteacher hero almost climaxes in an elopement, but comes to naught.

Independent heroines predominate in later noncollection stories, such as "Everything Happens" (1911), "The Neighbor" (1913), and "Lila" (1911). The first begins as the narrator rescues a young woman named Jeanette from street toughs in Paris. He lives with her for a while, but finding her "without a soul" decides to end the affair. His idea is to pass her along to a dilettantish friend as an initiation into sex. Jeanette, however, has something else in mind. She flings vitriol at the would-be lover, and ends up in prison.

Valentine Colignon, too, has a touch of the devil ("The Neighbor," 1913). When her husband is away, she sends gingerbread hearts to Tkalac, a young and foolishly chivalric Croatian fencing master, and raps on his window with a key tied to a string. If her object was to enliven dull married life, his is to make a grand, heroic gesture. No shamefully secret dalliance for the heir to castle Zvečaj! Let there be an assignation with all three parties present and accounted for! M. Colignon, thinking that Tkalac has come for a business loan, is amazed when the passionate Croatian lays his revolver on the table and states his real purpose. Madame, not at all happy with him for making her behavior public, tells him to "consider himself slapped." The put-down is complete. Tkalac arrows out of the room, forgetting his revolver, as the husband again offers his help, but now in a different tone of voice.

Finally, "Lila" (the title a nickname for Milica) tells of a lady bound to an impotent homosexual doctor. She leaves him. Moreover, she discusses his sexual problems with the narrator.

By today's lights, late-Matoš heroines like these appear more colorful than evil. Matoš, however, lived in times with a moral code which, for all his professed Bohemianism, he felt obliged to respect—in his fiction at least—even though he carped at certain strictures. Could he glamorize women without seeming to make Evil itself attractive? By the laws of Matoš's day, a seducer went free, while his victim was brought to book for waywardness. Premarital sex was all right for males, but for males only. No female should protest being passed along. That, too, was part of the code.[7]

But what if it were a matter of not perceiving female character correctly at the start? Here was a means out of the difficulty. The girl proves *not* to be what she seemed ("I Have Killed Her!"). She is another person ("Pretty Helen"); a minion of the Devil ("The Balcony"). There are exculpatory circumstances regarding her male partner ("Lila"). Or, wayward only for a short time, she redeems herself ("The Neighbor"). In the instance of Marta Gorska ("After a New God"), the reader is invited to behold a transformation: during an improvisation of Shakespeare's "The Tempest," she "changed completely into another person," and her face became "like that in a dream."[8] Her lover calls her variously Marta, Miranda, "Beloved." Indeed, Fanny and Alfred play the same game in "The Parrot," addressing each other as Venus and Tannhäuser.

Ultimately, of course, no female can escape fault. Woman is Eve, the temptress, the medieval *cloaca diabolorum* ("sewer of devils"). The girl next door is beset by provincial Don Juans, desirous of her body. Even if she puts them off, hers is the guilt for kindling their desire. In an early story, a potential victim connives with her husband to outwit a villain ("A Deceiver Deceived," 1895).[9] That is, surely, the *ne plus ultra* of a dutiful wife!

Since the moral code favored males, however ineffectual, women had to suffer them. Even though a woman paid the piper, she must always be deferential. Lila can climb into the impotent doctor's bed when she likes, but must take care to address him ever as "my dear little Doctor!"

Three stories of 1902 end in death. An impoverished student in Paris ("A Man of Conscience") has learned that he will not receive a much desired scholarship. Out on the town, trying to forget, he comes upon a young woman trying to drown herself. Despite abuse both physical and verbal, he rescues her; but, ironically, dies himself of exposure. Still unthanked, he goes to an anonymous grave.

In "A Light Went Out," a certain Count Andrija G. delivers a paper about what Lazarus saw in the world beyond. Exactly what he did see is never reported. Instead, the narrator—a gate-crasher at the soirée—reports the count's conversation with a young lady; his sudden fainting and hemorrhaging; his subsequent death. The count willed his earthly belongings to the church. Yet rumors circulate that his death is God's revenge upon an unbeliever.

"The Sparrow," finally, is the story of an eccentric doctor. In the past he appropriated other people's hats, to gratify a collecting mania; now he cherishes a pet sparrow. The bird is left with friends when he goes to England on business. They, however, serve it up for dinner upon his return. The doctor falls gravely ill, and all signs point to his early death.

Oscar Wilde once remarked, "There are few things easier than to live badly and die well." Though Matoš's characters die easily, they do not die well and the question arises: do they have any choice? The motives of the needlelike man, in the story by that name (in *Novo iverje*, 1900), are, at least, arguable. There is no doubt about the pregnant girl in "Mouse," from Matoš's first collection: she slashed her wrists. And the eccentric little doctor must perish because, in consuming the sparrow, he has eaten his own.

Death and life seem to have been, for Matoš, a continuum. In a late uncollected story, a dead man stands up and reviles his mourners ("Resurrection without Easter," 1909). The two nouns of the title derive from the same root. Elsewhere, too, the living converse with the dead.[10] In the early "Poverty" (1902), a Polish radical in Paris by the name of Grodecki is summoned to verify the death of a neighbor's child. During his visit, the mother takes poison.[11] Death lurks ever in the shadows.

What bothers Matoš is not so much the dying as the manner of it. The "man of conscience" and the fruit vendors end up in unmarked graves. The world goes only by appearances, a fact which can make for irony, as in the conclusion to "Mouse":

According to the world, the suicide was for reasons unknown; according to the uncle, it was because of Ljubica Kolarička. He was buried beside her and his aunt in the lonely Araberg Cemetery.

The deceased left behind a remarkable diary and the sketch of a dramatic poem in German.[12]

In fact, however, the death was an accident.

Sometimes, death resembles an intellectual separation; the dying person achieves a new point of view. "Path to Nowhere" is such a philosophic journey. Orlovič and Marjanović, two members of the Croatian gentry, meet in Paris, where they drink and talk over old times. Marjanović, feeling death near, produces a manuscript entitled "Path to Nowhere—Notes of a Journey to New America." His ideas are murky, but defend voluntarism ("To wish is to be able"). Pointing to a chart, he says:

> Those are the meadows of Nothingness, eternal absolute non-Being, as Spinoza defines it at the start of his *Ethics*. This nothingness of mine is eternal pure Being and, therefore, amounts to an eternal Positive—while what you call extension, appearance, matter (all your "nature") is a fiction, a zero. . . . I am personally and eternally one with the absolute idea.[13]

Marjanović wants to project his ego upon nature, to transform himself into pure thought and will. Suddenly, he flings the manuscript into the fire, thereby cutting his last ties with the world of people; now, at long last, he has become free. That night, he dreams of being slain by a vampirelike creature. Next morning, Orlović finds him in frightful condition and after making medical arrangements, departs for the Boer War.

IV *Other Aspects of the Stories*

Was Matoš a bigot? The evidence is conflicting. In "Sonata in D-Major" (1892), the second story written by him, the hero Salamon Rosenzweig rises from obscurity to become newspaper editor, lawyer, and politician. This youthful, sensitive spirit, fond of music and of poetry by Heine, once felt attracted to a young gentile, Dragica, who rejected him. Years later, with her father at a concert, she rejects him again, this time with considerable acrimony. Yet Rosenzweig goes on to defeat Dragica's father as a candidate to the national assembly and hears himself praised as a true Croatian, the pride of the motherland. Matoš's treatment is sympathetic.

Contrast "A Time to Remember." The curious Dr. Hagen, a professed archeologist and anti-Semite, is, in fact, a Jewish pervert with a fondness for wearing priestly vestments and playing at Catholic rites. Here he is, just before being unmasked:

> The archeologist had draped himself over Uncle Grga's armchair and was drinking wine from a venerable chalice. His bare legs, which resembled not so much X-rays as some O-ray yet undiscovered, rested on the crucifix of the *prie-Dieu*. A stole and dalmatic covered his lumpy back. Chuckling, he read from Grga's missal as if from the Budapest Caviar, with a black preaching-tricorne tipped over one ear.[14]

A little earlier, Hagen regaled dinner guests with anti-Jewish fare "more peppery than that in some rich Benedictine monastery." No one protested. The repertory of anecdotes was ugly—the Jew and the capon, the Jew and the pepper, Smuggler Jake and the robbers.[15] Matoš even coins a verb *jidlovati:* "to make ethnic jokes in Yiddish."

He understood anti-Semitism from his days in Paris at the height of the Dreyfus case; the disease was also rampant in Croatia. In his essay "Križevac" (1910), Matoš defends himself from any imputed discrimination. Yet he leaves the impression that he may be damning with faint praise:

> Despite reading in Voltaire, Dühring, and Renan, where Jews seem like intruders, I am not anti-Semitic. Enlightened Jews lose their undesirable characteristics. An ancient Hebrew spirit engendered the English Puritans, Milton, the unconquerably free-spirited Taylor and Carlyle. Heine, Marx, Lassalle were Jews in the manner of Old Testament prophets or Saint Paul, chief proselytizer of Christianity. The Hebrew mind is unoriginal—sterile and uninventive; but it is moral and ethical . . . sinewy, economical, practical. . . . The Jew is sober, extremely long-suffering and pious, in his element as head of the family. Not noted for courage, perhaps, but what matter is that?[16]

A certain amount of anti-Semitism typified the intellectual of Matoš's day. Worldly wisdom maintained that Jews controlled the Hapsburg press; that, in Croatia, they stood for commercial advantage and political repression and reaction.

Matoš depreciates all Orientals. They are lackeys, like the servant in "Among Strangers" (from *Novo iverje*, 1900), their nature crafty, their looks unsympathetic, their sallow skins evidencing jaundiced moral fiber. Any Greek was odious, as were Levantines in general. The rebarbative bureaucrat of "A Ministerial Paté" (from *Umorne priče*) is a Serb of Greek extraction living in Paris. He has taken to seducing young women—in particular, one named Nini, whom he abandons after two weeks. When they chance to meet again an ugly scene ensues, whereupon both are arrested. The Greek manages to wriggle out of it, leaving Nini in jail, then writes a letter about moral degeneracy in Paris. Matoš interjects this thought: "Like all Orientals or like any non-Muslim, he was greatly impressed by elegance and aristocracy. Yet he carried on without style. The same can be said for the run of Greeks, Rumans, Moldavian boyars, and Montenegrin princes in Paris."[17]

Not perceiving that Paris was a mixture of good and bad, high and low, the Greek attuned himself only to the worst and behaved accordingly.

The evening party setting, as in "A Light Went Out," is linked with imminent misfortune. Count Andrija lectures on Lazarus, but will die. At another soirée (see the uncollected "First Song," 1901), the heroine's love will, unfortunately, not be reciprocated. Obviously, then, the setting of "Ingratitude" (from *Iverje*) portends trouble. Elegant Afred Petrović, a secretary at the Austrian embassy in Belgrade, has maintained a background of mystery and is known only for his parties in the grand style. At one lavish affair, Alfred's parents arrive from the back country, and from their coarse remarks it becomes clear that the family wealth was ill-gotten: a friend (and benefactor) was swindled in the process. The party over, father and son brawl. The police arrive and take them away.

In all of these stories setting is of more importance than plot. We savor the ambience of "Ingratitude": taro games; the music of Mozart and Gluck; the chatter about Sir Arthur Sullivan and the art of Sir Lawrence Alma-Tadema; the writings of Max Nordau, Friedrich Nietzsche, Gabriele D'Annunzio; champagne, Rüdesheimer, liqueurs; caviar, mushrooms, *foie truffée*, oysters; a haze of cigar smoke, an aroma of the good life. It is a pungent, also mordant, description of society which Matoš was doubtless prepared to offer by having played the cello in small chamber ensembles at private soirées in Belgrade.

The scene in "First Song" features music by Schubert. The guests are a mixture of officers, professors, government people, handsome ladies in party dresses. Conversational cocktail-time sonar, with an occasional "Who is *that?*" eventually brings to the reader's attention Marjanović and Danica, central characters in the story. Meanwhile, the air reverberates with ideas. Marjanović, for example, opposes suicide to materialism: he believes that civilizations ought to be measured by their beauty, that friendship is more obligation than pleasure.

From the soirée it is but a step to literary portraits, such as "The Great Man" in *Tales from Weariness;* they unfold very much in the de Maupassant manner. Here, a pompous, role-playing Belgrade literary lion is summoned to Paris by his mistress, who pretends their idiot son is ill. He is shown a "corpse"; told that he has come too late; bilked of his money and sent away. What she has shown him was merely a doll.

In his absence fellow critics speculate why he might have left. Among them is Steva Banaćanin, who closely resembles the writer Stevan Sremac (1855–1906), a familiar from Belgrade days. Also present is one Šeširljić, a Swiss Ph.D. quite like the great man, his master, "in spirit and in Socratic schoolmasterly mien." Manfully he tries to legitimate the absence.[18] Šeširljić really delineates the Belgrade critic and professor, Jovan Skerlić (1877–1914), with whom Matoš was unfriendly. Finally, into the negative portrait of *on* ("he") himself, Matoš incorporated traits of Bogdan Popović (1863–1944), yet another highly regarded Serbian critic and esthetician. Surely Popović could not have relished the description of him as a literary Barnum without special talents; as a rice-bowl revolutionary and faddist; as a self-publicist; as a debater who argued only where he was, from the start, a self-proclaimed victor; and as one who in Paris played the Serb, and in Belgrade the Parisian.[19]

In the nostalgic "A Time to Remember," Matoš drew at least half a dozen portraits, which Tadijanović has worked out.[20] Perhaps the three most notable are Grga Alagović, who represents grandfather Grgur Matoš (1812–1899); Jurica Trumbentaš, in real life Matoš's boyhood friend and fellow cellist Juro Tkalčić (1877–1957); and Gusta Hajdukić, the poet August Harambašić (1861–1911). Matoš himself appears under the pseudonym Petrinović, a device, and a name he was to use later in the 1902 story "After a New God."

The description of the grandfather is both vivid and detailed. A giant of a man, when dressed in his ungirdled black caftan and cap he looked like an unbearded Moslem priest, a *hodža:*

He reeked of smoke and tobacco, like a just-emptied café. His left eyelid remained half-open, making him look distrustful and mischievous. His bluish nose was reminiscent of sea mushrooms or algae; and his smoke-filled nostrils brought to mind pitch on the bark of a peach tree. His face was puffy, as though his mouth were full of water; his thick eyebrows arched like a white vault above a cask in the cellar.

In conversation, he made me look into his eyes—eye, that is—and had a habit of touching the tip of my nose with his index finger: "That way, I know whether you're lying!"[21]

It is a portrait in which the author clearly took joy.

Many of the stories are little more than anecdotes. Sometimes these are strung together, as in "A Time to Remember." More often only a single incident is recounted. Interesting or humorous it may be, to be sure. But it is just barely enough to sustain the author's further opinions on topics like friendship or bureaucracy ("an intellectual proletariat") or insurance ("a lottery on human life"). Matoš built a repertory. He wrote folksily about a barber who wagered that he could cut off a corpse's nose ("A Terrible Wager," 1895); about corrupt village toadies who regale a very important person on his visit to Babindol ("A Skewer for His Excellency!" 1909);[22] or, in a story pattern as old as Homer, about the return of a stranger from Texas to a small Slavonian village, where he meets his lovely stepsister ("The Odyssey," 1895).[23]

When all is said and done, the most successful of his tales deal with types peculiar to the city. "A Matter of Honesty" (1901) tells about an aspiring regional accountant who finds fifty thousand florins of government money in the street and turns it in, for which action he loses his fiancée and some of his friends. After a time, he cannot stand these privations, turns to embezzling,and is jailed. Again, "A Life Worth Millions" (1909) describes how society fawns on a man of supposed wealth, and how the consensus changes when the rumor proves false.[24]

V General Comments

By his own appraisal, Matoš's stories had two merits. They embodied "social values," and were at the same time "stylistic studies."[25] If that was a bid to take sides, it was mightily successful. For those with sociological taste, Matoš provides references to anarchism or socialism, to Ibsenism or female emancipation, to social pathology and to venereal disease; he is *très à la page*. For the stylists, what matters is the man's relation to Edgar Allan Poe or Charles Baudelaire or Maurice Barrès; the formal and generic features.

The spoor toward stylistics was laid with mention of Poe. "I learned

most from him," Matoš said, though the lessons obviously came sec-
ondhand.[26] He agreed that a story should be concise, dramatic, and
realistic (in the sense of "well-observed"). Reality, of course, compre-
hended the uncommon, the improbable, even the bizarre; for that is
what Matoš's readers were thought to want most.

Poe's were stories of atmosphere and psychological analysis. But
while Matoš approved of the first, he disapproved of the second. Analysis was gratuitous. Symbols were the thing. The reader must see with
new eyes, understand in a new dimension. What the artist should do,
he told Milan Ogrizović in 1907, is "to refine and crystallize common
perception."[27] And he should also provide variety: "I think that every
story ought to be (pardon my emphasis) written differently, so that a
reader will exclaim: 'It cannot be the same author!' "[28]

The early stories favor a portentously unhappy viewpoint, but Matoš
was far from wanting to limit himself to tears. Like Heine, he preferred to weep *and* to laugh, not realizing that the combination might
work against him in some contexts. He is not consistently kind or subtle. He does generate his own brand of whimsy, especially when
recreating personal experiences, such as schoolboy pranks.

A delightful example may be found in the early pages of "A Time
to Remember." The schoolboys have been discovered in their efforts
to make "Goatgirl" drunk. Her father has put them into a shack with
an aroused billygoat, locking the door. The shack sits atop a cliff. Now
the narrator:

Chaos and confusion! Suddenly everything began to rock. A giant fist was
crushing us, like ants in a bag. I grabbed someone's leg. Something hit my
head. I saw saints and stars and seemed to be flying in the clouds. Finally, I
landed on grass beneath a tree. By the full moon I could plainly see a black
avalanche of chicken coop, pigsty, holding pen—whatever it might be!—
descending toward a ditch, amid a caterwaul of human and animal voices.
All at once a fellow sufferer came hurtling out. I rushed, that is, slid downhill
and collected my friends in the garden. The building hit the ditch like a shot;
another Whump! All bloody, our tormentor lay in the brook. The shack had
come to rest on his rib. We were about to rescue him when we heard a clomping of boots and a voice: "Wait, you thieves!"[29]

But the boys waited not a bit. They scattered into the surrounding
shrubbery.

Matoš brought to his work a zest for smells and sounds, a feeling for
milieu. Many isolated examples could be given, like the barking dog

in "After a New God," or the smell of old leather which permeates the priest's room in "Fresh Cracknels!" An extended sample can be cited, again, from "A Time to Remember," where Uncle Grga's library bedroom is a chamber full of visual, auditory, and olfactory delights:

> I awoke at dawn and washed and dressed quietly, so as not to waken the chaplain, who was breathing heavy and fast as though in fever. A lark flew in at the window and perched on a curtain, chirping as if to tell me something. A clock struck, the frightened bird fled. Cuckoo! It was the little Swiss house on the mantel. On its gates a clock, which showed 3:30; but a tiny Capuchin monk, a dwarf as it were, was striking 12:00 with a golden hammer on a golden anvil. The "book browsery" was, of course, commodious and full of mousetraps. Besides, it smelled of moths, Styrian eggs, quinces ripening red or yellow in heavy, dark, oak cupboards. In that grey room, my bed shone white, like pigeon eggs in an attic nest.[30]

Descriptions of the church and the parish house salon are similarly impressive.

One last example. The preelection mass in "For the People" (Matoš's last story) starts with a procession outside the church to the tolling of bells. It is a spring morning. As the churchgoers mill about in a landscape of lime, apple, and walnut trees, they are joined by Janko, the story's hero, fresh from his own little garden, where the air is steeped in roses and strawberries. Everyone is colorfully dressed: the schoolteacher's wife and daughter, the schoolchildren in short pants, varicolored vests and round, black hats, the parishioners, "smelling of drawers, chests, closets and washed linen." From Jakob Kohn's tavern, across the way, where a soldier is dancing, can be heard a little band, violin and bass fiddle, tamburitza and *berde*.

Once inside the church, the assembly is again described:

> There arose a stifling heat and a composite odor of sheepskin, slicker, boot polish and feet; the smell of poverty, of salt and old tobacco and old sweat; a stench to make the skin crawl, the eyes burn, the guts heave. It weighed on the chest like a millstone; an aroma of tallow, cheap hostelries, ashes, and damp, singed wool.[31]

Old women murmur rosaries, "their blue-gray lips clopping like hoes in parched soil." The collective prayers and pieties shake the church "as if blind hands were knocking upon the ponderous gates to life and death."

In an extensive study, the modern Yugoslav critic Ivo Frangeš has
considered the importance of musicality, rhythm, and repetition in
Matoš's style.[32] Lengthy descriptions, he says, are intentional and serve
the purpose of deliberately retarding action. Matoš continually exper-
imented, but did not always succeed. He wanted his narrative language to be different and variegated. Many readers would have preferred uniformity, however, since style sometimes gets in the way of
the story.

CHAPTER 3

The Essayist

MATOŠ'S major essays appear in *Ogledi* [Perspectives, 1905], *Vidici i putovi* [Look-outs and High Roads, 1907], and *Naši ljudi i krajevi* [Our People at home, 1910].[1] "Essay," as used here, denotes a short prose piece which states the author's views on a single subject and which cannot better be described as occasional piece *(feuilleton)*, review, or obituary. Incidentally, any essays discussed are given English titles; for original versions, see the bibliography.

The reasons for all that careful definition can be illustrated from *Ogledi*. It contains four genuine essays: "Stendhal" (1901); "Beatings in Literature" (1905); "Imaginary Journey" (1903), a fantasy return from exile; and "Barrel Organs" (1905), a laborious treatment of these instruments as symbols of civilization. But at least half of *Ogledi* consists of literary letters from Switzerland and France.

Vidici, too, is a farrago. There are essays on Janko Veselinović, Charles Baudelaire, Bishop Strossmayer, which readers of Matoš, a literary man, might expect. Also included is "At Home," important because it treats Zagreb as the patrimony of Dionysos and relates Croatia to the Greek classical tradition. In addition, there are trivial articles on Easter; home as a symbol; the nondramatic quality of contemporary life; and even (in "Siesta") some reminiscences of Belgrade.

Naši ljudi has half a dozen categories: (1) figure essays, like those on the storyteller Stevan Sremac, the Belgrade critic Skerlić, the Croatian poet Silvije S. Kranjčević; the musician Nikola Faller; and the impressionistic painter K. M. Crnčić; (2) literary essays ("National Culture," "Modernism," "Books and Authors"); (3) obituaries (Žarko Jovan Ilić, Vladimir Vidrič among them); (4) travel pieces (Lobor, Samobor, Rijeka); (5) book reviews; and (6) reminiscences (Matoš's flight from Zagreb in 1894; a portrait of his priest-kinsman Ante Pinterović).

The three books above are "collections," then, but take no account of polemics; art, theater, and music reviews; notebooks; or letters. Evidently, Matoš's bounty defies narow description. Attention is better

49

directed toward the man's images of himself. No one denies contradictions in the underlying principles. But, given the circumstances, the life becomes understandable.

I *Images of Self*

Matoš viewed journalism ambivalently. "There is nothing finer," he wrote from the Paris Exposition of 1900. And yet, upon reconsideration in "Books and Authors" (1907), journalism is commercial, superficial, and inimical to literature. He was a journalist despite himself, a man who wanted to live from writing, even when it did not pay well.[2] He needed a saleable image.

When he began to review the cultural scene in Belgrade in 1897, Matoš took stock of his talents. His goal was to supply pleasure and information. He soon cast himself in the role of a bohemian who knew everyone and everything, dashing about like a hummingbird among delphiniums. A provident hummingbird, who kept records of possible ideas (which he tested in letters to friends); who exploited coincidences and pseudo-events, while providing a sense of movement; who apostrophized people and favorite places, such as the Dardanelles Café. He really enjoyed performing and conversing, and he did both brilliantly. In the phrase of Tin Ujević, Matoš was "Holy Ghost of the café life."[3] Food, drink, tobacco, an audience were vastly stimulating to him. The Dardanelles became his office. This reporter who lacked a newspaper became now a literary lion, now an impecunious self-proclaimed victim of fortune's buffets.

Abroad, he played Don Juan. Letters from Switzerland and France mention affairs which remain inscrutable, probably because they never occurred. They were, though, beautifully reported, with an atmosphere of illusion. "When the great are not one's acquaintances, one sees one's acquaintances as great," Ujević has remarked.[4] Matoš may have known a few of the French working class; the words *grisettte, midinette, cocotte* recur in his letters. But, after all, he knew no one in high society. His closest friend in Paris was probably the postman.

Don Juan stressed his powers. "I can find a woman quicker than a piece of bread," he tells his father in 1902. There is much talk of affairs; Woman in general and women in particular. A rendezvous is imminent with a German governess from Munich, but Matoš lacks money to buy her coffee. He tags himself Matoš Gustafa, recalling an affair with a Belgrade chambermaid. He becomes a font of advice to young Vladimir Tkalčić, back in Zagreb, about married women ("What's needed there is boldness").[5] The ultimate proof of attraction was a gratuitous gift. In "Paris Chronicle" (1912), he describes how his lovely neighbor Janette Lévy ("blonde as the Doge's wife, golden as a sequin") voluntarily brought him soup and a crust of bread; he begged God to forgive her sins and let her into heaven.

Theorizing about love, he instructed young Tkalčić that a lover must retain certain illusions.[6] In a letter of 1909 he told Hilda Fürstenberg, a German translator of his work, that true love was innocent of duty and happiness: "Love is sweet until it becomes duty. At any event, I have observed that women generally experience love as happiness. . . . Love is not happiness, happy love is not true love. . . . Up to now, I have found love only in books."[7] Though Matoš was much involved with Olga Herak at the time, we find him harking back to the age of chivalry, for "Today, true love cannot be found, even in novels, because the so-called modern spirit cannot conceive it." Contemporary love had been impeached by journalism, degraded into eroticism.

One must decisively separate women from the woman issue (feminism). Don Juan agreeably notes the female presence; but at the mention of women's rights, his hackles rise. He stays with the *macho* tradition of his age. As early as August 1897, in a dispatch to *Nada* (in Sarajevo) he quotes approvingly from a book of aphorisms which he has just discovered in a Belgrade bazaar: "A woman is like a blind person who goes forward, even if she will stumble!"[8] In a recurring figure, the great Marko Kraljević, too, swung his club and cursed the vilas.[9]

The views of this writer are extreme. There cannot be sexual equality until men bear children. He does not like *les flirts* in Paris who represent the end of romantic love because they are overly concerned with status. Marriage may have become an institutional refuge *(Versorgungsanstalt)*, but not every man is ready for such an institution.

We take much of what he said as spoof. Certainly he did not, like Poe, see every woman as doomed maiden or dreadful revenant ("the mother-wife in her two aspects").[10] He professed Baudelaire's opinion that woman is either the temptress (Eve) or the saint (Beatrice). From this foothold he would strike out at woman intellectuals like Georges Sand, whom he called "the lustful Creole," aping the title of her book. He "rated" men, moreover, on how they perceived women and love and passion. Byron gets full marks, Rousseau fails; Stendhal (who understood only passion) and Heine (who understood only troubadours and *Minnesänger*) receive a qualified pass.[11]

In exile, it was natural that Matoš the Patriot should seek out fellow countrymen, especially students and artists. Many were, undoubtedly, socialistic, even radical. An anarchist appears in the first pages of the story "Among Strangers" (from *Novo iverje*), which is set in Geneva. Matoš, however, never intended to be a conduit for new social awareness. He more readily favored art than flag burning, and in Munich viewed the work of Leon Koen, a Belgrade artist. In Paris, at an exhibit of ethnic dress he affected annoyance that things Croatian were missing: "We Croats, too, deserve an exhibit. Ours would focus on that peculiarly native counterpart of Beau Brummel, the unknown and alas! unsung lawyer-*boulevardier* of Zagreb."[12] Croatia's cultural supremacy was indisputable, so he thought, and Matoš enjoyed thumping the drum.

The patriot has always existed. Young Matoš hurled insults at *Ban* Héderváry in Zagreb and at Janko Veselinović in Belgrade, running him down by comparison to the great Croatian novelist August Šenoa. *Amor patriae* emerged as a quality less clamorous but even more deeply felt when Matoš returned home, that is, in the years after 1908. He began to visit Croatian cities, extolling their glorious past as centers of heroism, ancient virtue, moral purity.

In "Samobor" (1908) he wrote, "Places are people; people are places," a thought which led to the title of his third essay collection (and even to the subtitle: *Portraiti i pejzaži* [Portraits and Landscapes]). There he takes another look at the patriotic poet Stanko Vraz (1810–1851). Though Slovene by birth, Vraz had had the eminent good sense to become Croatian; in fact, outdid himself by reading deep moral lessons in the flora and fauna of his adopted homeland. Matoš adds: "Nature is not merely an aggregation of [physical] forces but a picture, a symbol, a soul—for us, a Croatian soul. Environment—scientific, esthetic, moral—affects our will as well as our actions. Landscape is the chief source of Croatian energy."[13] He also admired Vraz for stressing the importance of a purely Croatian heritage. "Vraz was among the first to feel [distinctly] Croatian and to sense the dangers of a selfish Serbian chauvinism."[14]

In "Lobor," written the same year, Matoš wanders through a barren courtyard and contemplates a ruined castle as dark clouds rush overhead. Conversing with his shadow he again finds Croatia unlike Serbia.

Except for monasteries and royal places of pilgrimage, the Serbs "lack ties with the past."[15] On the other hand, the courts and ancient families of Croatia are a visible tradition which cannot be denied. Current ignorance about Croatian history is to be deplored; so is the decline of high heroes into court toadies. But, of course, in Serbia it is even worse. There the aristocracy has sunk to the level of merchants and tradespeople.

It is impossible not to add a few words about the essay "A Field of Nobility" (1913). The title refers to a site south of Zagreb near Luka-vec, the center of an ancient elective commonwealth known as Turo-polje, whose inhabitants had withstood savage assaults by Turks and by Magyars. The citizens foresaw danger in Illyrianism, both the Napo-leonic variety and the aesthetic brand promoted by Ljudevit Gaj in the 1830s. Deeply fearing dilution of their culture by aliens, in Gaj they discerned pro-German leanings.

The land bespoke August Šenoa, who had been married there in 1868. Even earlier, it served as the setting for "The Cannon of Turo-polje," his first story. The great man had imbibed whatever history and morality this place had to offer. "In his soul he knew all the *reliquiae reliquiarum* from time out of mind," as Matoš puts it.[16] Like a refrain—somewhat as he had done with on-rushing clouds in "Lobor"—Matoš keeps inserting the words "The lark soared high," a quotation from Šenoa's *Mladi gospodin* [The Young Gentleman].

Let no one forget the image of the Critic. Leaving Belgrade, Matoš elevated himself from reviewer to literary historian to theoretician. His essay on Stendhal appeared in *Ogledi* (1905), but dates back to Geneva days. The beginnings of a new critical outlook can be found in the letters "From Ferney" and "Cologny, December 1898"—the first covering Voltaire, the second, Byron.[17] They are trivial but instructive, and say something about Matoš in 1898.

What is new is the orientation. Voltaire and Byron are not Yugoslavs. Matoš, here, looks in new European directions. However good his French background, his English, unfortunately, tends toward the "howler" variety and is both primitive and comic. Somewhat unstyl-ishly, the letter from Cologny also cites Nicholas Lenau (in German) and Ovid (in Latin), and alludes knowingly to Dionysos, the harp of Aeolus, the Akropolis and Mt. Parnassos. The study of Voltaire dips into a Yugoslav stockpile (Pavle Solarić, Divo Bunić-Vučić, Petar Petrović-Njegoš), but also cites Condorcet, Brunetière, Brandes, Leo-pardi, Heine, and Goethe.

Both essays are so summary in nature that the reader gets the feeling of being crowded. Here, for example, is part of what Matos says about Byron. Note the multiple "firsts":

Byron's unhappiness goes back to being born in England and to marriage. His was the first great protest . . . against conventional wedlock. His life is the public tragedy of the male spouse, a glorious venture in "free" love. . . .

An unconsciously philosophical poet, he is a real-life revolutionary of the instincts; the first poet who dared to be free, individually and practically speaking. Byron's life is prologue to the philosophical individualism of Stirner and Nietzsche, to the dramatic individualism of Ibsen. He is the first free poet-personality.[18]

The rapid pace does not convey a feeling of depth.

There is superficiality too in the comparisons of Voltaire with Goethe: "Goethe the pagan, Voltaire the theist; Goethe unpopular, Voltaire adored; Goethe like Apollo, Voltaire monkeylike; the servile Karlsbad poet, the prophet of the French Revolution; the phlegmatic Frankfurter, the fiery Parisian—can there be a greater contrast?"[19] Another example of his juxtapositions involves Heine:

. . . Heine is most like Voltaire: the same inconsistent superficiality, the same acerbic, yet voluptuary temperament. Both ridicule the simple faithful, yet appreciate Catholic religious poetry. Both are satirists, but Heine's humor (although here and there with the Voltairean manner) is far more poetical. Heine is the greater artist, Voltaire the greater prose writer. Heine resembles Aristophanes; Voltaire, Lucian. Heine is the greater because, in all likelihood, [Voltaire's best puns] . . . were lost in the powder and merriment of Sans Souci or some other salon, while the thrifty Jew unfailingly put his perfected efforts to paper. Heine is the hero of pain and love and passion; Voltaire is the hero of thought.[20]

The technique of literary accountancy, when overdone, becomes stultifying. A reader feels foolish, having to see everyone as lesser or greater, and only Matoš seems to have a scorecard.

The essays do reveal a personal cachet. When Matoš introduces Byron, the effect is heavily first person: "There are great writers to whom I am indifferent, e.g., Alfieri, and others (like Tolstoy) to whom I am hostile. Among those I cherish are writers from my homeland— and Byron. . . . If I prove boring, it is not his fault."[21] Like Chuang-tzu, Matoš wonders: did Byron really exist, or did I invent him in a dream?

Descriptions are long and contrived. From Villa Deodatti, Byron's one-time dwelling just north of Cologny, Matoš offers this view:

> The village is huddled down to my left, in the [western] corner of the lake, between the Rhone and the hills. It looks dark and sad, as in the time of Byron or Shelley or when Stendhal noted that Geneva was empty and sad and lacking in monarchical graces. Above, hamlets, hills, and waters. A wavelike humming from the cathedral towers [of Geneva], as if the city of Calvin were sobbing in grief. Across the lake . . . the expansive, lofty Jura mountains, their bare spots yesterday patched with silver and gold . . . [they seem] the mighty wings of an unseen apocalyptic bird buried in snow and mist.[22]

The first thing that registers about this passage is its falseness as observation. If in school, Matoš would have been cautioned about purple passages. His thought-surrogates may add to the ambience, but contribute little to the substance.

II   *A Cultural Alliance*

Every small country faces the choice of affiliation or autonomy. In Croatia, the choice was aggravated by foreign domination and ethnic hostilities; the Croats were both anti-Hungarian and anti-Serb. As early as October 1894, Matoš had written from Belgrade to his brother Leon:

> I do not wonder now at the dreadful conflict between Serbs and Croats, being convinced that we are bound only by language. As to character, Croats and Serbs are different. A true Croat—and I speak of Croatia proper—is the man of a thousand years ago. Our heroism has spared us from foreign influence . . . while the Serbs [had to survive] Turks, "Rumans," Bulgars, and usurious Vlahs and Greeks. Small wonder these foreigners have left a mark and changed the original Serbian character.[23]

On such arguments he spends himself furiously, adducing data on names, skin and hair color, temperament. He could write less extravagantly about the Serbs, it is true, as witness correspondence with his mother, and also his remarks upon leaving the city in 1898. But no question of a cultural connection with Serbia ever arose in the mind of Matoš, that is clear.

Who would make a congenial partner? He suggested, by turns, Greece, Italy, and France.

Croatia enjoyed a long and honorable literary tradition, even if

Matoš believed that an ally was now needed. The stage was set early, as Mihovil Kombol puts it in a standard modern text:

When the Croats ... reached the vineyards and olive orchards of the Adriatic, they found themselves in an ancient cultural milieu which, from the earl Middle Ages, decisively affected their spiritual life. Understandably, the first lasting Croatian political and ecclesiastical organization emerged ... in Nin. Furthermore, Croatian literature begins in Littoral or Adriatic Croatia, well before the Turkish and Venetian conquests.[24]

The Italian Renaissance contributed to a flowering of Croatian literature in the sixteenth and seventeenth centuries, exemplified by Petar Hektorović, Marin Držić, Ivan Gundulić. The Baroque, colored by names like Zrinski and Frankopan, was succeeded by the rationalism of Matija Reljković (1732–1798) and the Franciscan, Andrija Kačić-Miošić (1696–1760)—then came a lull until, in the nineteenth century, national resurgence begins. Throughout, a separate history of folk literature existed. So, for a land that lost its independence to Hungary in the twelfth century (and later to the Hapsburgs), Croatia had much of which to be proud.

When it came to choosing a cultural ally, Matoš's first choice was Greece, and an essay in *Vidici i Putovi* states his case. Here is the opening of "At Home" (1907). The narrator, a former Zagreb resident, is introduced as he returns to his city after an absence of eleven years:

Martin out of Zagreb. Martin back to Zagreb. For eleven years now, I have not seen the city whose *kaj* is the sweetest sound in this world; a [similar sounding] word in Greek means "and" ... no wonder that we residents of Zagreb, like Socrates, avoid foreign tongues and love ladies who wear the costume of Venus. We, too, are classical, if not in the classical philologist's sense.[25]

The argument is restated at the conclusion when Martin, now in the company of Petrica Kerempuh, meets Dionysos who announces that Zagreb is his patrimony. Petrica was a pranksterish folklore figure, at once a patron saint of Zagreb and a Till Eulenspiegel, supposedly kinsman of a seer named Grabancijaš. Matoš punned on the sound pattern when fictionalizing himself as Petrinovič in several stories. Furthermore, the contemporary Miroslav Krleža (1893–) used him in a series of poems ("The Ballads of Petrica Kerempuh," 1936) which trace Croatian history.

Martin wants Dionysos to lead him to ancient Athens. The present is becoming ever more stupid and incomprehensible. New inspiration, a new prophet is required. The essay concludes with Martin's prayer to Dionysos, a part of which says:

> . . . let the souls of our public speakers pass into swine! You who may make a prophet from a jackass: turn our prophets into jackasses! . . . May this wine embolden us to reach the sun and your soft moon. And, like the blessèd Paris, Anchises, and Adonis, may I, too, look upon beauty. Impart to me the dream of Ocean, which comes through the Gates of Horn, and in sleep instruct me, oh great eagle, in the art of poetry which alone is the bliss of dreams and forgetfulness.[26]

Here the argument rests, with the same touch of playful humor as at the beginning.

In the original version, differently titled when it appeared in *Obzor* in 1905, the whole is fantasy (perhaps the ultimate evaluation of the Greco-Croatian theory!). What worked against it from the start was Matoš's antipathy to modern counterparts of Paris, Anchises, and Adonis. He simply could not abide Greeks, Levantines, and Orientals. As Ujević remarks: "He found [them] ridiculous."[27] He was even suspicious of their long names.

The essay contains an original poem, loosely modeled on Verlaine, with the opening line "Duša moja čaroban je kraj" ("My soul is an enchanted country"). Matoš later bestowed on it the essay title, "At Home," and published it separately. Of interest is the final stanza, a picture of backward rural life:

> Duša naša zagorski je kraj,
> Gdje jadnik kmet se muči zemljom starom
> Uz pjesmu tica, kosaca i zvona.
>
> O, monotona naša zvona bona,
> Kroz vaše psalme šapće vasiona:
> Harum—farum—larum—hedervarum—
> Reliquiae reliquiarum.[28]

> Our soul's bourn lies beyond the hills,
> where the sad peasant toils on the ancient
> land to a song of birds, scythes, and bells.
>
> You monotonous, sickly Croatian bells! The
> universe whispers through your pealing:
> Harum-farum-larum Hédervárum! Here the past
> never changes.

The last two lines, leaving aside the reference to Ban Héderváry (1883–1903), are meant to suggest a medieval heritage which goes back to Rome.

Catholic Croatia looked toward Rome. The Serbs were orthodox; Catholic, but of the Eastern rite. It was authority, as well as common faith, which sealed the bond. Even avowed agnostics and anticlericals like Matoš acknowledged the church as a force. His father August (1847–1914) served for thirty-five years as organist of St. Mark's in Zagreb. It was a Roman Catholic bishop, Strossmayer, who founded the original Yugoslav Academy of Sciences in Zagreb, and his name remains part of the city. Ante Starčević, founder of *Stranka prava* (Faction of the Right), was an ex-priest turned politician.

The most explicit statement of affiliation was "From Rome" (1913), a series of articles for *Obzor* and the by-product of a visit to get medical help. "Salve, Dea Roma!" ("Hail, Goddess Rome!"), the opening piece, contains this passage:

> Rome, eternal goddess! Although Croatian, I am a Roman citizen! Our finest sustenance was suckled from the Roman wolf, and until 1848, our Diet spoke the idiom of the [Roman] senate. Although no longer Latin in language, we qualify in spirit, will, patriotism, orientation, and love of freedom. . . . Sixtus V, our own blood, gloriously served as pope. . . . Our Starčević, *ultimus Romanorum*, steeped himself in the classicism and patriotism of Livy, Tacitus, and Plutarch. We have dearly earned the right to Roman citizenship; and in our struggles against Germanic and Pannonian barbarians, now just as then we seek refreshment in the eternal youth of a reborn classical spirit.[29]

Matoš's tribute was not unlike that of predecessors like Byron, Stendhal, and Goethe.

Roughly speaking, however, he put modern Romans and Venetians in the same category as modern Greeks. They were parodies of the ancients. Italian culture was mediocre, pastalike. Futurism combined sensationalism and success; it was a literary *Barnumština*, with dangerous militaristic overtones. Italian politics also repelled him. On a visit to Fiume (Rijeka) about 1909, which he describes in *Naši ljudi i krajevi*, he finds "an unhappy, stolen city," thoroughly and truly Croatian. Vestiges of the past may be few, but he is almost gleeful to note an absence of traditional Italian culture.[30]

An alliance with France? Why not? Matoš was, of course, predisposed toward French culture by reason of acquaintance and residency in Paris. France, after all, had inherited the Roman classical tradition. Moreover, modern France was the home of the symbolist movement, which Matoš admired. Here, too, lived Maurice Barrès.[31]

France's defeat at the hands of Germany in 1871, especially the loss of his native Lorraine, had splayed Barrès's affections. Despite intellectual allegiance to Goethe and Nietzsche, he rejected German culture in favor of Rousseau and the skeptical Ernest Renan, once his teacher. He looked southward—not only toward French cities like Aigues-Mortes (the setting of *Le jardin de Bérénice*, 1891); but toward the Spain of El Greco (*Du sang, de la volonté, et de la mort*, 1894 and *Greco ou le secret de Tolède*, 1911); and toward Italy, birthplace of the romance spirit (*Amori et dolori sacrum: la mort de Venise*, 1902).

Barrès, whose political life links three nonvictories (defeat of Boulangism in 1889, defeat of conservatism at the second Dreyfus trial, and defeat of Rhenish annexation after World War I), spoke for a cultural minority who were both antidemocratic and antimaterialistic and who wanted desperately to worship heroes when there were none. His message, first and foremost, was an affirmation of Self, but not merely in a promotional sense. Faith in oneself was necessary in a cruel and degenerate world. Isolation, communion with one's own feelings and instincts, would replace rationalism and social contacts which had lost their meaning. "Intelligence—what a little thing on the surface of ourselves!" he liked to observe. Barrès wrote beautifully. He took pains to publicize his image as a recluse; an eccentric who shapes his mores according to his thinking; a romantic traveler.

Another aspect of Barrès was the superpatriot. *Le jardin* celebrated Bérénice as an unspoilt yet traditional type among the French people: that fact was more important than the book's refinement, hedonism, even its eroticism, because it foreshadowed Barrès's nationalism. He entered politics, serving many years as a member of parliament. He glorified his homeland and its past greatness, as exemplified by Napoleon. He philosophized about Power, Will, Violence, Truth-to-Oneself, and other dangerous abstractions. Primarily a psychologist and moralist (at least, from Matoš's point of view), he subordinated all to his religion of the homeland.

Yet his patriotism had a distinctly local twist. He made much of geography and soil as influences on character, striking a note reminiscent both of Taine (landscapes as *états d'âme*) and of German National Socialism *(Blut und Boden)*. He spoke of a mystical Energy, which was the soul talking to itself in a natural setting. Usually, the center was Lorraine. In *Les déracinés* (1897), he describes the sad results when seven Lorrainers are uprooted and arrive, disoriented, in Paris. (One of them has an imaginary conversation with Taine.) In the end, all are reunited at the tomb of Napoleon. The funeral of Victor Hugo is also described.

But perhaps the best illustration of the philosophy is *La colline inspirée* (1913), an attempt to demonstrate the tribal or atavistic vitality of native soil—here, as always, in Lorraine—at Mount Sion/Vaudrémont, a monastery. Three priest brothers of peasant origin (Léopold, Franjo, Kvirin) are inspired to establish a heretical cult. They desire a church "grown from the soil," not one of foreign origin. In their need, they are aided by an ex-priest from Normandy named Vintras. All are imprisoned and excommunicated. But, in the end, Léopold makes peace with the church and is buried with churchly honors after the Franco-Prussian War. The author suggests that paganism and church all serve the same purpose: "The church, too, comes from the field (nature) and is nourished by it—so that we may be free."[32]

We are all products of tribal or social development, and of milieu, and we embody ancient elements which can be evoked, either from ourselves or from our surroundings. Just as the Catholic faith everywhere contains folksy, earthy ingredients, so does the Lorraine of the novel contain reminders of earlier days: cocks (instead of crosses) in the church towers; ruins of a temple to the Celtic goddess Rosmertha.

In Croatia, says Matoš in a review, there are also places where an ancient wind blows, evocatively: "Our Croatian homeland, too, has places where the spirit prevails—a fact known to our elders, such as Dimitrija Demeter and Stanko Vraz. The beautiful native solitudes whisper eternally of God, the people, the past; of duties toward our leaders and our dead . . . yet few of us feel Croatia to be a bulwark (as in the past) or can match how Barrès felt about France."[33] These forces vegetate among the people, even if too few perceive them. The novel is "a hymn to nature and to home places" where local spirits and voices can be detected. We are their product, and landscape is a way of conversing both with them and with ourselves.

Matoš never credits Barrès with being a great thinker. Rather, he reflects a general European crisis: that of nationalism versus cosmopolitanism, especially critical in the instance of a small country like Croatia. Above all, he is interesting. Note that the first criterion is good writing; writer before nationalist. Even so, questions linger in Matoš's mind. How could Léopold make his peace with the church, surrendering to authoritarianism and centralization? Matoš finds it unconvincing. He will acknowledge only that *all* religions contain *something* natural. "Religion is nothing more than the touch of an unknown, mysterious, and extremely subtle Nature upon our souls. . . ."[34] The religious sentiment is both natural fact and spiritual condition.

Apart from Barrès, French culture as a model was simply a case of the nearest and best. Matoš never specified what form his cultural alliance would assume. One can imagine his recommending a program to include closer acquaintance with French authors; but, fundamentally, it is French standards of literary practice which interest him. Any Matoš program would contain these points at least:(1) Expression: A writer must demonstrate a feeling for language, a talent for expressing himself. Matoš himself was extremely subjective. But subjective or not, a writer must write well. (2) Range: Not only should material be researched and assimilated, but opinions and judgments ought to be put in a context of general European literature. In other words, range should be broadened. (3) Permutation: Raw imitation of French models is not enough. Alien themes and models must undergo changes in a Croatian environment—otherwise, Croatia will lose its literary identity. Every Croatian writer is, at the same time, a patriot and nationalist. More detailed explanations of Matoš's ideas are given in the sections which follow.

He was not fully qualified to judge the Paris scene, much as he might enjoy it. Marijan Matković likens him to a "provincial bumpkin" or a child at a bazaar.[35] He lived in a Paris of impressionistic painters, but prefers to deal with dead academicians. He cannot accept Manet for being too radical. In literature, he quite overlooks André Gide and Romain Rolland and changes his mind about Barrès (from negative to positive). Zola (or Zola's naturalistic school) he could not abide. No theorist, he was a paraphraser, an eclectic; but that did not prevent him from being doctrinaire where poetry was concerned. He insisted that the only models to imitate had been provided by Frenchmen in the

late nineteenth century, and he lectured poets like Dučić and Rakić
for not following them. But then, Matoš himself did not always follow
advice.

One idea which he almost certainly took away was that criticism is
literature—it is not psychology, sociology, ethics, or politics—and must
be judged accordingly. Aesthetics precedes all else, even logic. True,
Matoš spent much of his life writing out of his field. He could accept
errors. But let someone else use language carelessly or violate one of
the Matoš canons (no matter how antiquated)—he would be on the
spot with his literary whip, applying lashes where he felt them due and
often striking twice in the same place in order to increase the pain.

III   The Essay on Stendhal

"Stendhal (Henri Beyle)" was written during the Geneva period, but
was not published until 1901, when Matoš had long been in Paris. The
essay illustrates his favorite devices. It is full of quotations, including
poetry by Đura Jakšić (1832–1878) and Silvije S. Kranjčević (1865–
1908). It is biographical in approach and personal in manner. But typ-
ically, like most of his essays on foreign authors, it lacks substance. Quotations abound from Nietzsche, de Musset, Renan; but they are superficial and have little bearing on the thought. Matoš is merely showing
off and being, at the same time, enormously unoriginal.

He chronicles Stendahl's birth in Grenoble, his death in Paris; his
acquaintances (Napoleon, Byron); his physical appearance. Biography
was to become the hallmark of the Matoš method, on the premise that
a man's life and work are inseparable; the one is a clue to the other.
So, biography became part of a standard format: life—work—summing up.

Small wonder, perhaps, that a man who started with the personal
side—and whose whole literary manner was nothing if not personal—
would soon be accused of excessive spite. Branimir Livadić, an editor
of *Savremenik* and an author in his own right, told what it meant to
be on the receiving end of Matoš's criticism: "A few swipes at style,
followed by philologizing, advice-giving, rewriting, deceptive quotations, jokes. Then, bang! 'The book is bad, scandalous!' "[36] The poet
Jovan Dučić or old Janko Veselinović could probably provide variations on the technique. Matoš imprisoned the former in outdated metrical restrictions and accused the latter of having written himself out.

In a letter from Paris to Andrija Milčinović, a friend and fellow author, Matoš writes: " . . . the friends of Dučić say I am hateful and personal. As if ideas and men could be separated; as if I could hate a work without hating its author!"[37] Most often, whether the critical assessment was positive or negative depended on style. Poor style meant poor ideas, a rule that brought criticism even upon the great Stendhal, whose style was nothing if not legalistic. All artists, by birth, enjoyed a superior sensibility; but they must cultivate superior expression. As Matoš puts it in "Books and Authors": "A literary man is not only feeling, he is style."[38] Alas, his care did not extend to contents. How easy to dress up a void!

The great weakness of "Stendhal" is its emptiness. Matoš mentions every fiction, travelogue, or essay that the author ever wrote; he provides schematic summaries and facile generalizations—to no avail. Obviously, the information was extracted at second- or thirdhand, and Matoš tries to cover up with stylistic tricks, wordplays, and quibbles. Stendhal was "simultaneously imaginative and reflective," the reader is told; his imagination was reflective, his reflection imaginative. He analyzes "excessively"—Matoš disapproved of analysis—yet was "insufficiently objective." Soon the words do not matter. The reader tires and turns away.

In the end, the man fascinated Matoš: his self-concern, his contradictory mixture of Don Quixote and Hamlet, his dabbling in new fields. Since he saw the goal of life as naked power and favored the exercise of will, Stendhal found it easy to preach revolution. With one sweep he would abolish democracy, a coup that suited Matoš, for whom the word was mere rhetoric. Yet beneath his armor Stendhal dreaded ridicule and did not actually participate in the revolutionary causes he so readily championed. His aim was ever *to seem what he was not*. In the final analysis, guided by an inner voice, Stendhal knew and trusted only himself. Matoš found him a predecessor of Barrès.

IV *The Essay on Baudelaire*

There was considerable difficulty getting "Baudelaire" published. After three rejections it appeared in the short-lived *Jadran*, run by a friend of Matoš in Trieste, in a version quite different from that in *Vidici i putovi*. It follows the format of "Stendhal," with which it has other ties.

Baudelaire, like Stendhal, interpreted the world in highly personal terms. Although any personal or inner vision (along with its nonconformist externalization) would have attracted Matoš, Baudelaire had, in addition, spoken for a symbolism which Matoš himself adopted and which underlay the whole idea of what it meant to be modern. According to Matoš, every modern artist was a Baudelairean. All his life, the French poet searched for cosmic symbols to communicate the inner light. To put it another way, his neo-romanticism was opposed head-on to realism or naturalism, two other movements of his day. He glorified the city as against the countryside, so far as *any* dreadful metropolis of mid-century could be "glorified"; and he cared not a fig for nature. His world was Paris in all its aspects, sub- and supercivilized. Hypertrophied civilization was, in fact, a recurrent theme.

Baudelairean art accepted life as raw material only. Reality was not a "slice of life," but a refined end-product. Nor was the natural superior to the artificial. Nudity counted for nothing; clothes made the man, a fact well understood by Beau Brummel and other dandies. Cosmetics enhanced nature, enabling plain women to become beautiful.

Baudelaire's philosophy appealed to Matoš on several grounds. Baudelaire measured life individually—that was also Matoš's sentiment. Society provided little hope; Matos felt that "true progress lay only in perfection of the individual."[39] But what about the Baudelairean *spleen*, the poet's elevation of unhappiness and pain? That, says Matoš, was a fact of life and Baudelaire deserved praise for putting it to aesthetic use. Man's goal, after all, was "to experience cruelest pain as sweetest pleasure." If Baudelaire was an interesting poet, what matter if he cultivated suffering and chose symbols such as black cats?

In a verbose summary, Matoš mined picayune comparisons and confidently totted up his account. There is praise for "Tertullian nobility and moderation" of style, for being "a Manichaean with strong Catholic tendencies." If *that* did not confuse the readers of *Jadran*, Matoš added that Baudelaire encompassed "Shelleyan pantheism, cabalism, the wisdom of Scotus Erigena and of Dionysius the Areopagite. . . ."[40] To the end of his days, he felt that the essay was greatly underappreciated.

V *Essays on Style and Home Talent*

The nucleus of Matoš's criticism is his notion of style. Nowhere is this concern better illustrated than in the essays of *Naši ljudi i krajevi* [Our People at Home, 1910]. In "Books and Authors," an essay of 1907 already mentioned, he argues that a writer's first responsibility is "thor-

ough comprehension . . . of his native tongue."[41] Every Croatian
author, he says, is a defender of homeland and language. Of course,
culture—here synonymous with fine art and literature—may have
international themes. But, he contends in "National Culture" (1909),
there must also be a national stylistic manner, unless "Croatian culture" is either to disappear or to become very much diluted. Worried
about influences not only from abroad, but from within, he staunchly
resisted anything which could be called Serbian, Serbo-Croatian,
Yugoslav, or even Slavic; and deplored the cultural Illyrianism of the
past.[42]

Several factors worked against style. One was journalism, which
prized quantity and speed. Another was the absence of a practicing
cultural élite in Croatia. In Matoš's view, "modern" should not be
equated with "new" or "chic," but with "a way of thinking and living
shared by the élite of Europe."[43] Croatia simply was not a modern
land. Then, the decline of romanticism, entraining a loss of individualism, also boded ill because, for Matoš, individualism and artistic
excellence were one and the same. Finally, de Maupassant, Zola and
Tolstoy were pernicious, representing as they did factionalisms. When
people became debaters, they lost a certain stylistic freedom. Art, after
all, was to be judged on purely aesthetic grounds.

Style is the real theme of two further essays written in 1907. "Jovan
Skerlić" is an attack on the Belgrade professor and critic, who had just
begun to publish the series *Pisci i knjige (Books and Authors)*. Skerlić
was a moralist, a socialist, and a nationalist. Adverbs like "soundly" and
"sensibly" rolled easily from his pen; he approached literature system-
atically and with definite preconceptions. With his love of clarity, he
felt closer to eighteenth-century rationalism than to nineteenth-century romanticism; his assaults upon romantic writers infuriated Matoš,
who regarded them as attacks on individualism and, therefore, on style.

Matoš acknowledged their temperamental differences, though with
ill grace. He blamed Skerlić for running him off *Savremenik* and
besmirching his reputation. (A letter from Milan Ogrizović in September 1906 had described a conspiratorial meeting in Sofia where Skerlić
criticized Matoš on several counts, including immorality.)[44] He would
repay the account, in spades. In 1903 he disparaged Skerlić in a story,
calling him "a Swiss Socrates." Now he reached into the pot and drew
forth new epithets like "Tatar Cassius." He questioned Skerlić's foreign-language background and dismissed his doctorate as second-rate.
It was entirely *ad hominem:* "We are different poles. He is the social-

ist; I, the nationalist. He is, or claims to be, Yugoslav; I am Croatian. He is a realist, I am not. He, the professor; I, the Bohemian. He preaches, I mock."[45]

When Matoš speaks about taste ("the benchmark of worthwhile criticism"), his real topic is style; for "criticism . . . is the study of style."[46] It is also, however, the study of people—their similarities, but especially their original and distinctive differences. Regrettably, when Matoš compiled a critical inventory, he felt bound to include any personal traits which were disagreeable to him.

By way of digression, it is interesting just how far Matoš would go. Style is more than mere literary scholarship, he informed Bogdan Popović (Skerlić's teacher, the self-acknowledged "father of modern literary criticism") in 1912. It transcends the requirements of clarity, he advised the aged Ljubomir Nedić in 1901, for "style [is] Reality."[47] Matoš assigned it a metaphysical status surpassing all mysteries, demoniac or otherwise. According to him, aesthetic truth might be independent of mundane fact or material existence. In other words, the fantastic (yet "real") characters of Edgar Allan Poe and Nathaniel Hawthorne were, from an aesthetician's point of view, superreal.

The second of the 1907 essays was addressed to Milan Marjanović, author of *Synthetic Criticism,* which becomes the title of the essay (in *Naši ljudi i krajevi*). Marjanović wanted to define modernism within Croatian life as a whole. Skerlić had erroneously associated art with socialist doctrine; Marjanović now associated it with what Marx would have called "the relations of production." According to Marjanović, style depended upon the relationship of author to reader, and upon subject matter.

Matoš could not but regard such thoughts as diabolical: "What devil goaded Marjanović into thinking that style is determined by reader and subject? Style improves with distancing from the public, with minimal concessions to 'gratifying' content."[48] Certainly, immaturity and perverseness in an audience are deplorable. And, of course, one can humanize an author through biographical details, anecdotes, and reminiscences. Yet the values upon which style depends are originality, beauty, and suggestiveness; and they are absolutes.

The essays on Stevan Sremac (1906) and Silvije S. Kranjčević (1908) also deal with stylistics when Matoš does not get carried away with other concerns. Sremac was an old friend and patron who, unfortunately, lacked the Matoš kind of expressiveness. He used regionalisms and nonstandard borrowings to describe Serbia's Turkish and Muslim past. For all that, he also symbolized old Belgrade days, this urbanite specializing in rural village life and humor. As of last memory, he shuffled around, coffee cup in hand, "like an old waiter," dressed in a red-belted grey robe. The essay is an interesting example of Matoš's self-exploitive manner. For the readers of *Glas Matice hrvatske*, he dredged up memories of "his (other) friends" Janko Veselinović and Simo Pandurović and of good times back in the Dardanelles.

If Sremac was someone whom Matoš liked *despite* his style, Kranjčević was a case of disliking both man and work. The poet had just died, and the occasion was observed in two essays: "For Kranjcević" appeared in *Hrvatsko pravo;* another version ("In the Shadow of a Great Name") found its way, first into *Savremenik*, then into *Naši ljudi i krajevi*. In a 1901 letter to his friend Andrija Milčinović, Matoš confessed to finding the poet uncongenial—great moral revolutionary though he might be. In correspondence with young Vladimir Tkalčić in 1903, he classified the style as "unappealing" and "affected." Kranjčević was as selfish as he was pessimistic.[49]

Yet now, he praised Kranjčević for a "Croatianness" which brought folksongs to mind, making light of the fact that he was a relentless moralizer, an old-fashioned and rhetorical neurotic. Yes, it would be well, were there more poetry and less philosophy. Certainly less cosmic gloom. But Kranjčević had, after all, remained well within the Croatian tradition as a patriot who lauded laborers and loved children. Despite his fiery Byronic spirit and his Baudelairean *spleen*, this man was a solid Croatian. Unconvincingly, Matoš calls him "our best."

The later Matoš is vulnerable on the question of patriotism. Once he had said (of Maurice Barrès) that the writer came first, the nationalist second. Now he suggests that much can be forgiven (to Kranjčevíc or Vladimir Vidrić or August Harambašić) by reason of birth. Without doubt, he preferred Harambašić (1861–1911) above all the rest as man and poet, even fictionalized him agreeably in "A Time to Remember" (1900). However cheerful and patriotic, Harambašić was a middling poet. Yet on grounds of patriotism, Matoš chooses to overlook the failings in the work of this bland love poet, this amiable political hack. About the only thing Kranjčević and Harambašić shared was that they lived close to the gun all their lives. Suicide and the madhouse were never far away. Perhaps in addition they shared the burden of keeping literature alive in a land which cared little about poetry.

Matoš was never impersonal, and as he aged, became increasingly strident and ponderous, more and more ill-humored. All things considered, he achieved most when he wrote about himself or about Zagreb; when, whimsically and unpolemically, with stylistic dash yet with seeming innocence, he cast his spell and created his art. The personal touch was a hallmark.

Characteristically, he suggests intimate acquaintance with those about whom he wrote. But, evidently, not everyone knew him to the extent he would have the reader believe. The poet Vladimir Vidrić, for example, is familiarly addressed as Lacko ("In a Yellow House," 1909). Yet Matoš thrice missed seeing him when alive; and the reader should discount the closeness suggested by physical details, such as the poet's large, dark "feminine eyes." Matoš also may have known Nikola Faller, a Zagreb musician who is the subject of a study in *Naši ljudi;* but Faller did not know him, addressing him by the name of his father, August.[50] In the obituary of Žarko Jovan Ilić (1906), the situation is different. The humorist Žarko was the son of Jovan and the brother of Vojislav, both poets. The supportive details (sickliness, stomach disease, alcoholism, chain-smoking) seem convincing, the anecdotes incontrovertible. But the more important aspect is that Matoš again succeeds in drawing attention to himself:

I saw him only two weeks ago, sickly as ever. That did not concern me, for (as Voltaire says) the healthy die while the sick recover. Since the death of his famous father . . . we had seen less of each other. He lived off in Palilula and was unwilling to give an address. Recalling the hospitality and the carefree atmosphere of life in the family house . . . I felt that he was [too] ashamed and embarrassed to let me into his new life, surrounded as he was by poverty and weak female relatives.[51]

Matoš comes on strongly as the old family friend. After all, was not Žarko in the habit of calling him "Gustika, the cantor's son"?

VI *Zagreb, City of Dreams*

Zagreb was to Matoš what St. Petersburg was to Pushkin and Gogol. In 1900, it numbered some sixty thousand inhabitants. Matoš continuously celebrated his city: its ethnic elements, antiquity, buildings, and food. In the essay "At Home" (1905), he lists Zagreb specialties like buns, crescents, egg or honey cakes, cracknels, and crêpes. He speaks of Zagreb as dear, accursed, mundane, servile, bureaucratic. White-washed official buildings occupy places where he played as a boy.

"Zagreb Singular and Plural" (1912) mentions Grič, Kaptol, the Lower City, and says that much of the city's charm depends on the contrasts among them.

Many portraits in *Naši ljudi* were Zagreb people, like the musician Faller, the senator Đuro Deželić. But Ante Pinterović, a cleric and cousin, lived in nearby Brezovica. The essay on him first appeared (1910) in *Hrvatska sloboda* and described in loving detail this strong, tall man with small grey eyes and large nose, this "classic example of a Croatian parish priest," who lived with several cats and a housekeeper sister.

Yet Pinterović is not the real topic, only a vehicle. Matoš relives his school vacations: "Never have I found a roof nearer to heaven, or where the beat of rain was more agreeable. There, among attic rummage, I first discovered a spider-webbed edition of Kant. . . ."[52] Memories pour back through the years: playing big brother to the parish children, helping the sexton, going on picnics, bathing in the Sava, crabbing or rabbit-catching or sparrow-shooting or cockfighting. There were parties in a great park nearby, magnificent sunsets over the Samobor hills, moonlight on sedge and pond. He fell in love with the local postmistress. Life was lordly and complete. When, a military deserter, he last saw the old man in 1905, together they watched Venus rise in the western sky and Zagreb, a patch of light, glistened amid the hills. Pinterović was worried about national leadership.

Matoš, too, fretted about Zagreb's ability to lead. It was not, with its foreign influences and alien aristocracy, a truly Croatian city—the countryside was more typical; that is where a cultural revival had occurred. Also, Zagreb lacked landed wealth. Nor was it a political or commercial center (like Belgrade, for example). As he remarks in "Social Life" (1910), an essay in *Pečalba*, Zagreb lacked even society and social dialog. There were groupings and cliques, but they were due mostly to alcohol or the café life. Salons were nowhere to be found. Nor did women enjoy a place in the scheme. "Zagreb is deficient in people-values and work-values," he wrote.[53] It was ruled by "Mr. Stupid" and his colleague "Mr. Mob."

Who would want to live in this city, affordable only to the rich or to residents of Mirogoj cemetery? Matoš, for one. Whatever its faults—no matter how superficial or profound—Zagreb offered prospects of renewal because it drew upon a collective past. "Famous places spark alert minds," he once said, and the feelings described in the following passage may well be his own:

"Walk up to Grič at night and, as if from a mysterious phonograph, you will receive the message of city, soil, people; you will experience the spirits of Grič: kings and *bans*, traitors and martyrs, sinners and saints."[54]

From this reservoir, surely, Croatia would be revitalized.

Two 1913 essays, posthumously gathered into *Putopisi*, deal with aquatic Zagreb, a rare aspect of the city. In "By Land and Sea" he readily admits that Zagreb is only fancifully a seaport; it is, as he says, "a seaport for people of imagination." But he describes various water-side sun-worshipers and swimmers (whom he calls "Indians" and "Fish"), before visiting the Zagreb Fair to view the paintings of Ljubo Babić. In "Along the Sava" he also observes men and women bathing ("men look best naked; women, dressed or half dressed"), but digresses into memories of how once while swimming he lost his clothes to a gypsy; or got locked into a pool in Switzerland.

These essays demonstrate more than an ability to focus upon him-self. A born mimic, he liked (as he told the suspicious policeman in "At Home") to "peek through the keyhole of language." So, he created new words—here, *Neptunopolis* ("city beneath the sea") and *vodo-holizam* (a portmanteau pun from *voda*, "water," and *alkoholizam*, to suggest "a passion for water"). He could accelerate or deliberately retard the pace, sometimes awkwardly with apostrophes or purple patches: "Flow on, flow swiftly, oh Sava, our swift and beautiful river!"

Much of his "observation" is spurious. "Several cows trudged into the stream, their large, peaceful eyes mirroring the silvery water and bringing to mind the paintings of Paulus Potter or Rosa Bonheur or some English landscape artist, while below the hill the Zagreb houses and churches showed white like a mottled flock of birds." One would have to be next to the cows in order to verify those details. The refer-ences to art are suspiciously general. And, though he used the figure on more than one occasion, what have white houses to do with mottled birds? Any description from afar should put the reader on guard. "Far off along the shore, a peasant woman or gypsy undressed with awk-ward modesty and slipped waist-deep into the Sava. . . ." The reader concludes that nothing much is happening, but that Matoš prefers a good show.

He could rarely avoid outrageous comparisons or jokes, even if wholly inappropriate. Possibly, however, that is one reason why his light ephemeral pieces worked. In them his humor is, by and large, effective. There are awkward spots, of course. But one excuses much in a writer who can be so delightfully whimsical.

CHAPTER 4

The Poet

MATOŠ's current reputation rests in poetry—a curious fact, considering his narrow output of perhaps 100 poems, mostly sonnets. He had trouble in finding a publisher. With high hopes he approached the Society for Croatian Writers as early as 1911. But the first major collection did not appear until 1923, nine years after his death.

Thereafter, his fame continued to grow. Six editions preceded the *Sabrana djela* [Collected Works] of 1976—testimony to a power to fascinate even beyond the grave.[1] Editors like Antun Barac and Dragutin Tadijanović became interested, although Barac, by the way, did not wholly share the current estimation. Writing for *Savremenik* in 1919, he found Matoš "a strange mixture of sincerity and emptiness, deep esthetic instinct and superficial virtuosity, warmth . . . and lasciviousness."[2]

I *Poetic Development*

Matoš explained his interest in verse as due to a writer's cramp which hampered journalism and music. Poetry, he said jocularly, entailed less writing; yet it satisfied both his ear and his literary bent. The years after 1906, especially 1906–1909, were fruitful for poetry.

Apart from a juvenile Petrarchan sonnet addressed to his schoolmate Dragica Tkalčić in 1889, and a poem tucked into a letter from Belgrade to his brother Leon in October 1894, the first published verse was "A Nocturne from Hrastovac," originally part of "A Time to Remember" (in *Novo iverje*, 1900). Although composed in Paris, it sounds very "Croatian," in large measure because it is written in *kaj-*dialect. The eight lines tell a lover's loss:

> Kaj da počmem, moja draga mati,
> Smrt i betek—to je sinek tvoj.
> Strelili su mene Smiljke zlati

Prami, Smiljka—to je betek moj!
Već je zorja, a ja nemrem spati,
Po hiži me hinca mislih črni roj,
Kokotiček već kriči za vrati:
Hajči, Smiljček, hajči picek moj![3]

How can I begin, dear mother, to tell you of my sickness unto death? My golden-haired Smiljka, she is my sickness. Dawn. I cannot sleep. Dark thoughts like bees follow me through the house, while a cock cries at the gate: Sleep, sleep, Smiljka my chick!

The poem has its own charm, apart from the story. The alternating ten- and nine-syllable (feminine—masculine) lines are well handled. The trochaic rhythm is confident; the rhymes are exact—he concerned himself with preciseness; and (except for an awkward inversion in the line third from the end) the verse moves along naturally.[4]

In the May 1905 issue of *Savremenik*, he published a gruesome sonnet, "Consolation from Her Tress," using the trite idea that death is sleep. The form is not what a student of Shakespeare or Milton might expect: *a b b a   c d d c   e f e   f g g*. Yet it is a base for future variations such as:

	a b a b		*a b b a*		*a b a b*		
		or		*or*			for the octave,
	a b a b		*b a a b*		*b a a b*		
	c d c				*c c d*		
and			*or*			for the sestet.	
	d e c				*e e d*		

The tendency is Italian. Certainly, there are no English quatrains with concluding couplets, and gnomic summing up is absent, in any event. For him, the sonnet was adaptable, not hidebound. He used it according to his lights.

His first major poem appeared in the November 1907 issue of *Hrvatska smotra*. "To a Little Girl in Lieu of a Toy" originated in a furtive Christmas visit to the Ogrizović family in Zagreb. Although reference is made to chestnut trees in front of her house, little four-year-old Ljerka Ogrizović, the dedicatee, was not of an age to remember the exact circumstances.[5]

No matter. It is interesting that an adult takes time to chat with a little girl; that the adult is Matoš in a rarely objective self-appraisal; and that even if the young girl/doll/dove does not comprehend, the reader gets the point at once:

Ljerko, srce moje, ti si lutka mala,
Pa ne slutiš smisla žalosnih soneta,
Kesteni pred kućom duhu tvom su meta,
Još je deset karnevala do tvog bala.

Ti se čudiš, dušo. Smijat si se stala
Ovoj ludoj priči. Tvoja duša sveta
Još ne sniva kako zbore zrela ljeta.
Gledaš me ko grle. Misliš—to je šala.

Al če doči veče kad ćeš, ko Elvira,
Don Huana sita i lažnih kavalira,
Sjetiti se sjetno nježne ove strofe.

Moje će ti ime šapnut moja muza,
A u modrom oku jecati će suza
Ko za mrtvim clownom iza katastrofe.

Ljerka, my darling little doll, sad sonnets are not for you, still ten years away from your first ball; your world is bounded by the chestnut trees before your house. You may well wonder and laugh at this mad tale; your precious soul cannot yet imagine how oldsters talk. Your dovelike expression says: it's all a joke.

But some evening you will recall these lines, like Donna Elvira weary of Don Juans and false gallants. When my muse mentions my name, a tear will start in your blue eye, as for a dead clown after the event.

There are no rhetorical questions, no props, no mythological tinsel.

An unusual poem from these years is the narrative "Mora" ("The Nightmare"), a 290-line survey of Croatian history from the time of the Zrinskis (seventeenth century). The poet dreams that he has been buried alive and that demons are tormenting him. When at last he awakens to the ticking of a clock, he realizes that death is only an abstraction and begins to take comfort in thoughts of his garden or the sight of people going to work.

Besides, Matoš criticizes various modern "isms" (imperialism, militarism, scientism), but especially belabors hypocrites and *Fachidioten* ("learned idiots"):

> Oružan mir—oj, davor, davori!
> Doktorski diplom u džepu bedaka,
> Bludnici stari s licem crkvenjaka,
> Sifilis progres i kulturne bijede,
> Napredan narod slaboga što jede. . . .[6]

A world of weaponry—oh, gods of war! A doctoral degree in the pocket of a fool, oldtime sinners with clerical faces, gains against syphillis [but] cultural losses, progressive nations devouring backward ones. . . .

His is an inventory of evils, without beginning or end; and wherever one looks there are more—not merely to be seen or read about, but to be smelled: "the crippled morality of urban cynics, / the delightful odor of expensive clinics." In the array, high and low, new and old, mythical and real are thrown together: doctors with fools, Bismarck with Chingis Khan, Jupiter with Buddha. Matoš likens himself to Philoctetes, who though possessing the arrows of Herakles, was bitten by a venomous snake along the route to Troy. The Davor here is the ancient Illyrian god of war, a word still serving as a personal name.

In a famous couplet, he proclaims himself "a scrofulous ulcer / borne on a mad storm."[7] The poet's interest in language is mainly zestful, however. "The Nightmare" is a metrical catalog song. The difficulty in this *mille e tre* is that Matoš wants to swat insects with bludgeons. His virtuosity truly dazzles: the varied breaks, the shifting number of syllables per line, the alliteration. But the doggerel is only a tour de force which brings to mind the annual name-rhyming pieces which Frank Sullivan used to do for the *New Yorker*.

He returned to Zagreb for good in 1908. Thereafter his interests narrowed. In a sonnet of 1909 ("To Young Croatia"), he reaches out to his juniors in a bid for leadership:

> Naš ukus samo rijedak dojam bira
> I mrzi sve što sliči frazi i pozi.
> Tek izabranom srcu zbori lira
> I nije pjesma koju viču mnozi.
>
> Naš stih je život koji dušu svira.
> Što može reći proza, dajmo prozi,

A strofa treba magijom da dira
I budi u nama ono gdje su bozi.

U vijeku, kada "misli" svaka šuša,
Mi, nimfolepti, skladno sjećajmo,
Jer cilj je svemu istančana duša.

Ljepoti čistoj himnu zapjevajmo,
Božanski Satir kad nam milost dade
Za cvjetni ukrs hrvatske Plejade!

Our taste selects only the rare concept, disdaining phrases and postures;
our lyre speaks only to select hearts, not to multitudes.
Our verse is life, soul music. Leave the rest to prose! By magic, poetry must
awaken our divine afflatus.
In an age when every imbecile "thinks," we lovers of art must serenely
feel our way toward spiritual refinement.
A hymn, then, to pure beauty! And may the Divine Satyr grant rebirth of
a Croatian Pleiade!

In this artistic credo, Matoš states that poetry is created by and for
the few and that care must be given to language, especially to its con-
notative and musical aspects. He appears to endorse private, even cryp-
tic, communication. But how rare *is* a "rare" concept? How deeply
may an artist withdraw into his own symbolism?[8] Matoš never answers
those questions.

II   *Matoš and the Tradition*

Croatian tradition extolled love. Good romantic/neo-romantic prec-
edent favored anonymous ladies with Grecian names and floral attri-
butes. Had not Robert Burns written about a "red red rose"? Goethe,
about a "Heidenröslein," along with much specious wisdom? After all,
life entailed loss of innocence. Flowers had secrets known only to lovers. Children stood closest to ultimate truth. Matoš's very first poem
concerned a flower, and between 1906 and 1914 his titles include "The
Pansy" (1907) and "A Secret Rose" (1908). (Also "floral" are "Mystical
Sonnet" and "Correspondences.")
If Croatian literature also favored patriotism, it was because, in
Matoš's day, no writer lived by belles lettres alone; literature was an
adjunct to politics. The reading public relished stridency, and Matoš—

fortunately, one might say—had inherited factional genes. In life as in literature, he scarcely knew the meaning of nonalignment, being incapable of lasting loyalties and quarrelsome by nature. For example, he owed his amnesty to the Frankists and contributed for a time to their organ, *Hrvatsko pravo*. The amity was not of long duration, however. He soon quarreled with old friends like Milan Ogrizović (who ran for parliament). Again, he scoffed when the poet Harambašić took a political desk job, although when Harambašić died in 1911, Matoš managed to laud him as "Croatia's most patriotic poet."[9]

A most useful motif was foreign domination. In "The Nightmare," Ivan Zrinski (1654–1703) suffers the name Gnade to prove that he lived "by the grace" of the Hapsburg court. In "At Home" (1905), cited above, Croatia is depicted as an economic backwater, an alien land where enslaved peasants labor, while the poet dreams of dead heroes and extinct noble houses. Sometimes, from exile, Matoš waxes purely nostalgic. "In the Grass" (1909) evokes a rural scene with nightingales and larks, dusty roads, ripening grain, church steeples poking into blue sky, laundry drying on fences. But usually, he takes the view that the land and the cities are being exploited; Zagreb is a nest of Magyars, Jews, and Serbs.[10]

The effect of foreign domination is that people become stupid and barren, a point twice made in 1909 (See "An Old Song" and "Dialog in Grič"). In the latter, a young *kaj*-speaking girl, just at bedtime, asks her father why *Croatians* never get to be *ban*, why titles and money always wind up in Budapest? The old man simply replies: "Hush, Bara! We are unlucky!" Ivo Andrić admired this poem and cited it as representative of Matoš's thought.[11]

III   *Matoš's Contributions*

In their anthology of Croatian poetry, Slavko Mihalić and Ivan Kušan mention the "close bonds" which link Matoš to French culture.[12] Olga Grahor devoted an entire book to this very idea.[13] It is only commonplace to say that Matoš was much influenced by symbolism in Paris. Surely, his ties to Baudelaire, Verlaine, Mallarmé, and Laforgue were important; and the French connection is, no doubt, a basis for his reputation at home. But what exactly did he bring back? How can it be demonstrated? How original was it, after all?

Lest there be misunderstanding: specific borrowing is not the issue. Tin Ujević accused his mentor of plagiarizing only prose. Similarities aside, little would be gained by matching Matoš's "unknown woman" to Verlaine or his "Mrs. Moon" to Laforgue.[14] Rather, one looks for the new orientation, the different direction which Matoš provided in Yugoslav literature.

What and whom did he know? 1900 was far from being the Great Poetic Year. Baudelaire, Verlaine, Mallarmé, Laforgue were all dead; thus, firsthand acquaintance was out of the question. But, even dead, each of these poets had something still to impart: Mallarmé, a concern for music and sound; Verlaine, for bohemian life and languorous landscape. Yet it was Baudelaire and Laforgue who most influenced the poetry he would write.

Baudelaire was a font of knowledge. As Elaine Marks has observed, *Les fleurs du mal* (1857) expressed all modern man's anxieties—exile, voyage, lost childhood; eroticism, sadism, revolt; the artificial paradise of drugs and alcohol. In her words, when it comes to "neurotic, urbane sensibility," Baudelaire is both Alpha and Omega.[15]

The gist of Matoš's essay, already mentioned, concerns the metaphysical status of symbols. (I shall use "symbol" and "metaphor" interchangeably.) As Matoš put it, "the basis . . . is pantheistic." Everything was symbolic, even clothing, which was " . . . not merely a defense against weather, but a mark of social position, often of status and temperament."[16] According to Baudelaire, the most effective metaphors showed an inner connection between things or between senses. Colors could sound, sounds could smell, smells could shine.

Both men wrote poems with the title "Correspondences." Baudelaire/ pursued his idea of linkage: "Les parfums, les couleurs et les sons se répondent" ("perfumes, colors, sounds answer one another"). Odors recall the flesh of infants; others bring to mind oboes, green prairies, rich musk, incense. By comparison, Matoš's "Srodnost" (1911) is pallid. His lily of the valley, growing under a willow by an old mill, is "innocent, white, pure as a child . . ." and, predictably, suggests his sweetheart. It is mere convention, the flower symbolizing moral purity. There is nothing of the French poet here, nothing internal or profound.

Baudelaire gave Matoš fresh ideas about setting. His Paris lacked ethnic enclaves and friendly neighborhoods; nor did the old medieval *communitas* prevail (as Matoš liked to think it still did in Grič). The city consisted of estranged, alienated, and insecure individuals.[17] Thus in several of Matoš's city poems it is dog eat dog. Nowadays a beggar gets no alms in the city ("The Beggar"). A husband slays his deceiving wife and is hanged for it ("A True Story"). A coquette changes lovers,

receives a beating, and dies in a cold Parisian hospital ("A Ballad").
Upon consideration, even Zagreb's Grič could become "a nest without
a falcon," a place of fogs, shadows, shabbiness, dead people, and aliens.
New settings, new urban characters—how about urban "music"?
Should our poet dip into Verlaine's "Art poetique" for the "grey song"
which was both cosmopolitan and earthly? No! for further help Matoš
turned instead to Jules Laforgue (1860–1887).

Laforgue wrote with sharp strokes and shifting moods. He is generally known for an irony which could run to sarcasm, a self-deflating
humor, a mosaic vocabulary, a mock-heroic or at least mixed manner.
He early cultivated a capacity to shock, to fix Prufrocks on pins. A
chronic jotter, he filled voluminous notebooks with quotations, comparisons, anagrams, and puns.

In "Archilochus" (1909), Matoš employs Laforgue's technique of
bizarre juxtaposition. German titles are bestowed on Greek goddesses:
Fräulein Psyche and *Blaustrumpf* Athena (Athena Bluestocking) are
both *besetzt* ("crazy"). Quarrelsome, queenly Hera is degraded to the
level of "whining" Xantippe, the shrew-wife of Socrates. A chaste
(Roman!) Vesta somehow has stumbled into this Greek company; here,
too, is Archilochus, famed for lampooning the daughters of Lycambes
when his suit was rejected. Another jarring note is struck by the col-
loquial expressions *s boljim [se] svijetom mlate* ("run around with the
better set") and *mlati gloginje* ("labors in vain," literally "whacks
down the berries"). Here is the piece in its entirety:

> Gospa Hera ko Ksantippa svili,
> Frajla Psiha Kupidona voli,
> Afroditi soldati su mili,
> Djevičanstvo Dijani se moli.

> Previše me blauštrumpf je Atena,
> Nimfe ljube—znate već—kravare.
> Ja pak nisam tako luda bena,
> Da zbog vila odem u svinjare.

> Sve s Olimpe dakle lijepe dame
> Il su bezect, il se kao Vesta
> Odnošaja s umrlima srame,
> Pa mi tako, nesrećniku, nesta

Svake nade za protektorate
Kakve čiste muze i lijepe boginje:
Te se ženske s boljim svijetom mlate,
Pjesnik za njih samo mlati gloginje.

Lady Hera whines, like Xantippe; Fräulein Psyche loves Cupid; Aphrodite prefers soldiers; young virgins pray to Diana.

Athena is too bluestocking for me. Nymphs, as you know, go for shepherds. But I'm not dumb enough to start a piggery because of some lady fairy.

In short, all pretty female Olympians are either crazy or, like Vesta, ashamed to socialize with mere mortals.

So, unhappily, I expect no pure muse or ravishing goddess as a patron: these ladies hobnob with society and look down on poets.

Via Matoš, Laforgue's monosyllabism passed into Serbo-Croatian poetry, along with a new embodiment of Lord Pierrot. Again, it was not that the Croat specifically copied the Frenchman; rather a case of lessons learned. Laforgue's "Complainte de l'oubli des morts" contained verses like: "Les morts / C'est sous terre; / Ça n'en sort / Guére" ("The dead are underground and hardly ever emerge"); "C'est gai, / Cette vie; / Hein, ma mie, / O gué?" ("This life is gay, is it not, my dear? Shall we go?").

Matoš learned well. In "Metamorphosis" (1909), eleven of the fourteen lines end monosyllabically, as Matoš contrasts the lordly vehicle of Zeus with a lowly meat animal. Even more starkly, he describes a bull fight where an inattentive matador is gored: "Ko u snu / Krv i bik, / Grozan krik" ("As if in a dream: blood, bull, wild screams"—"A Beautiful Death," 1912).

Erudition and colloquialism: that combination identified Matoš to many. He sometimes postured as "one with a childish heart who suffered deeply." But through Laforgue's influence he more characteristically gave the impression of being, in the phrase of Tin Ujević, simultaneously "from the salon and from the saloon" ("jednako ličan i uličan").[18] To put it another way, he may have had a heart, but he also had teeth that could bite.

IV   Other Aspects

The many variants suggest indecision. But two late sonnets from a mature hand also suggest great care and workmanship in stitching together words, lines, and sounds. In "Autumn Evening" (1910), the

reader looks out at dusk upon what appears to be a not unusual scene:
river, clouds, trees, hills, and gathering shadows. But the apple tree is
"proud" and the darkness "opaque," and the reader eventually comes
to understand that as day becomes night, life becomes eternity:

> Olovne i teške snove snivaju
> Oblaci nad tamnim gorskim stranama;
> Monotone sjene rijekom plivaju,
> Žutom rijekom među golim granama.

> Iza morskih njiva magle skrivaju
> Kućice i toranj; sunce u ranama
> Mre i motri kako mrke bivaju
> Vrbe, crneći se crnim vranama.

> Sve je mračno, hladno; u prvom sutonu
> Tek se slute ceste, dok ne utonu
> U daljine slijepe ljudskih nemira.

> Samo gordi jablan lisjem suhijem
> Šapće o životu mrkakom gluhijem,
> Kao da je samac usred svemira.

Clouds with leaden dreams above dark hills; uniform shadows on river
water which shows yellow between bare trees.
Cottages and a steeple somewhere behind moist meadow mists; a wounded
dying sun watches sombre willows blacken like ravens.
It is dark, cold; in early dusk, dim paths merge into blind human disquiets.
Only a proud apple tree, the seeming sole survivor in creation speaks of
life to the opaque gloom, and drily rustles its leaves.

The poem is tied together not only by alliteration and end-rhyme,
but by grammar and morphology. *Snov-* and *sniv-* (in line 1) are
grades of the same root. *Snivaju—plivaju* and *stranama—granama*
are grammatically parallel. The parallelism suddenly comes to an end
in the second stanza: for, despite appearances, *sutonu—utonu*, *suhi-
jem—gluhijem*, and *nemira—svemira*, are not parallel. Matoš builds
an effect of susurration and murmuring (in the final stanzas) with sibi-
lants *(s)*, grave consonants *(k, m)*, and grave vowels *(o, u)*.

"Nocturne" was Matoš's last poem, written and proofed only days
before he died, for the April 1914 issue of *Savremenik*. Shortly before
dawn, a sleepless poet listens to the stirrings of life:

Mlačna noć; u selu lavež; kasan
Ćuk il netopir;
Ljubav cvijeća—miris jak i strasan
Slavi tajni pir.

Sitni cvrčak sjetno cvrči, jasan
Kao srebren vir;
Teške oči sklapaju se nà san,
S neba rosi mir.

S mrkog tornja bat
Broji pospan sat,
Blaga svjetlost sipi sa visina;

Kroz samoću, muk,
Sve je tiši huk;
Željeznicu guta već daljina.

A tepid night; from the village: barking, a late owl or bat. A love flower:
the strong, passionate fragrance celebrates a secret feast.

The music of a tiny cicada makes a silvery whirlpool; like dew from the
sky, a peacefulness descends on heavy, nodding eyelids.

The somber clocktower tolls the late hour; blessed daylight streaks the sky.

Silence, as the muffled roar of a railroad train fades into the distance.

In tranquillity, he acknowledges that life will continue without him;
that in the end all will fade into eternity, like the sound of the train.
The rhyme becomes feminine and trisyllabic, as if compliant with the
mood. Again, the color shifts toward grave at the conclusion.

Note the imagery. For the most part, "Autumn Evening" was visual.
Here, the images are auditory: the poet *hears* the bell, the train, the
other sounds. He separates himself from them as physical things, and
they now exist in his imagination. Only the daylight is seen. The rest
is heard, smelled, or felt.

Quite different are the brief narratives which Matoš based upon folk
patterns and to which he gave a very personal twist. "Two monks once
met . . ." *(Sastala se do dva kaluđera):* that normally might introduce
an epic tale of derring-do. But "Acts of the Apostles" (1912), it turns
out, is a poem about two *non*monks (or non-apostles) who defraud an
innkeeper, gamble, carouse, and (after a brawl) slip away into the
night.[19]

Another folk vein was metrical wisdom of the proverbial sort, such as:

> Teško vuku koga vrane hrane,
> A junaku koga žene brane;
> Teško braći koji se ne slažu,
> A vojniku zaspati na stražu.

Hard for the wolf nourished by ravens, hard for the hero defended by women. Hard for brothers who disagree and for the warrior who falls asleep on guard.

or: "Lako ti je situ benetati, / A u proleć kencu zarevati" ("Easy for a well-fed man to babble and for an ass to bray in spring").

Matoš puts these patterns, too, to new use, taking shots at fashions of dress and marriage, for example. Dresses are costly and impractical. Besides, the poet adds:

> Blago onom kom je sudba slijepa
> Punu kesu i bogatstvo dala,
> Kad si fina, odgojena, lijepa.
> No kad nemaš dosta kapitala,
> Ostat ćeš na rosi, jer tek bene
> Užimaju bez miraza žene.[20]

Blessed is he to whom blind fate has given a full purse and riches. You may be delicate, well brought up and attractive. But without money you will be left out in the dew, for only fools marry women without dowries.

His tour de force in this direction must be "The Buffoon" (1910), based on a single rhyme:

> Teško je kad imaš mnogo duha,
> Još je teže kada nemaš kruha;
> Teško sluhu kada je bez uha,
> Teško uhu kada je bez sluha. . . .[21]

It is hard when you have an excess of spirits, still harder when you lack bread; hard for a rumor not finding an ear, and for the ear that doesn't find a rumor. . . .

It is also hard, he goes on, to take a word like *ruha* ("clothes") and
make it rhyme with *ćuha* ("breeze"), *stuha* ("fairy"), *gluha* ("deaf"),
and Petrica Kerempuha, the *genius loci* of Croatia.

V   *Concluding Thoughts*

How curious that Matoš remained an implacable enemy of blank
verse, for (as Jure Kaštelan pointed out) prose pieces like "Shadows"
(1908), in *Umorne priče*, come close to being just that:

> Sve, sve, je sjena.
> Svijet je sjena.
> I sunce je sjena mističnog sunca.
> I život je sjena tajnovitog života. . . .[22]

All is shadow. The world is shadow. The sun, too, is the shadow of a mystical
sun. And life is the shadow of a secret life. . . .

More consideration should be given to Matoš's poetic prose; to his rep-
etitions of words and rhythms; to his fondness for colors and flower
symbols. The tempo of his stories is sporadic, each burst of activity
sustaining a lyric digression.[23]

How tragic that he could so waste himself on the trivial! Matoš's
image of himself as a "dead clown" in the sonnet of 1907 (see above,
page 74) is largely successful. But elsewhere, when the theme was
patriotism or motherhood, he let himself wallow in sentiment. The title
of his poem, "Lady Mary," refers ambiguously to his mother, his
homeland, and the Holy Virgin. Too often style came before substance.
Too often he was satisfied with stereotypes.

As Tin Ujević justly observed, the poems call to mind cheap picture
postcards: the obviousness of the poses brings into question their
authenticity and sincerity. That was the real "catastrophe" suffered by
Matoš the poet.

CHAPTER 5

Summing Up

THOSE trying to pin Matoš on a phrase are doomed to failure. Tin Ujević, Ivo Andrić, Velibor Gligorić, Olga Grahor, Marijan Matković, Tode Čolak, Mirko Žeželj—no chorus of unity there.[1] The first two look out upon their subject as if from separate stars. Ujević thinks of Matoš as contradiction, "a Gothic spirit behind a classical phrase," a journalistic mouse behind a literary lion.[2] Andrić dwells on the Dionysian enthusiasms, the devotion to beauty, the spectacular style. "Matoš played with words like a child with pebbles."[3]

Since 1914, the criticism has changed almost with the decade. Interest lapsed with the postwar advent of expressionism. During the 1930s, a revival centered on separatistic aspects of the philosophy; even, unfortunately, on Matoš's compatibility with fascism. His mother received an honorarium from the state. Again consigned to Lethe after World War II, he emerged *poeta redivivus* in the late 1950s.[4]

I A Viewpoint

Mirko Žeželj writes, "The main goal was to bring together his life and his writings."[5] But it is nearer the truth to say that the two were never apart. He did not separate his *own* life and work; nor did he do so for Voltaire, Byron, Stendhal, Baudelaire, or anyone else. Journalist and man of letters were one.[6] Critic, storyteller, and poet were but three aspects of Matoš-Trimurti.[7]

Scholars and the reading public (insofar as they are distinct) have gone separate ways. By and large, scholars study the work; readers, the man. Scholars scrutinize the parts. Readers prefer the whole. In this atmosphere, Matoš has become both classic and unread. Scholars seem to prefer him dead, while the public, recognizing one of their own, accept him in one or more of the roles he evolved—Don Juan, Patriot, or Bohemian. There is even an Omnibus Matoš, the consummate social commentator, the incarnate Petrica Kerempuh, the Croat's Croat. He

85

has become a street in Gornji Grad, a plaque at 10 Jurjevska, a room at the Institute for Literature.

Gligorić describes him as a stylist.[8] According to Čolak, his style is "pithy, emotional, sensitive, and impulsive."[9] Grahor is concerned with French qualities; Žeželj, with Croatian. For an American reader, however, such points are of little consequence, since he will be looking through a telescope from afar and his question will be: is the man interesting? For a nonnative, style is an insuperable barrier.

Matoš's literary legacy consists of poems, stories, and essays. Perhaps a half dozen of each deserve to be kept, along with his letters. The rest—the polemics, theater-music-plastic art reviews, notebooks—are easily forgotten. Matoš must be reviewed by the contemporary reader whom he could not have foreseen. Will the real Matoš please stand up?

II Some Difficulties

According to his own testimony, *Vidici i putovi* traced an evolution "from anarchy to . . . subjectivism."[10] Whatever else these words may mean, they allow for inconsistency, a word which he often rationalized as "variety." *Are* the larger turnings of his life really excusable as demonstrations of integrity? Why would a friend of Janko Veselinović (or André Rouveyre or Stevan Sremac) not speak softly, even compromise a few principles? Why not merely remain silent? How genuine is a tolerance which includes anarchists in Paris, but excludes Jews, Greeks, and Orientals in Croatia?

He was no literary system maker. His theories hang neither together nor separately. While he berated others for imperfections of rhyme and form, his own ideas could be fatuous. How ironical that some of the prose can effectively be presented as free verse, when he remained, his life long, its enemy! He over-zealously awarded firsts. The epithet *najhrvatski* ("supremely Croatian") went not only to Šenoa, but to Kranjčević and Harambašić as well.

His is the charm of suggestion and mood. Impressionistic to the core, his descriptions often incorporate something distinctively personal—a new angle, a rare detail, the bizarre. He converses with his shadow, a black cat crosses his path, fancifully a room full of emeralds and rubies is dynamited, he sails off to Utopia in a balloon—such contrivances made his readers exclaim, whether in joy or exasperation, "that is Matoš!"[11] No one matched his captivation.

Ever in full career, he seems unconcerned about the gaps. He distorts or errs through ignorance. In the notebooks, names and quotations are misspelled.[12] Yet his vocabulary is so arcane that it requires a gloss, even for Yugoslav readers!

Is he an embarrassment to posterity? His *élitisme*, construed with the politics of the 1930s and 1940s, does not sit well. Since his Croatia was, essentially, a figment, perhaps he should be regarded as less culpable. But can one rely on his judgments even about that figment? Matoš advocated relentless retrogression and few of his religious or social positions can be generalized. His Croatia was a Balkan Spain, replete with groves of oak. Not even his symbolism can withstand prolonged exposure.

III   *Man and Work*

Images of the wanderer recur. In the stories, the narrator may be a lonely journalist, photographer, or artist (as in "Pretty Helen"). The presiding intelligence of his letters from abroad is a traveler; even his last book title *(Pečalba)* conjures up a migrant day laborer. Travel became a way of life which, all in all, suited him well. "He wanted to understand life as poetry," says Gligorić.[13] Travel was a form of poetry, and poets traveled better than others because they detected enchantment in extraordinary places. Landscape was music, he told Milan Ogrizović in 1907.[14]

"I am strongest when alone." That quotation from Ibsen's *Enemy of the People* might serve as his motto. Solitude became his literary aura, his mystique. Solitude helped him to generate what Daniel Boorstin has termed "the pseudo-event": a little thing made to seem more important; an event which did not occur at all; an illusory motion. Don Juan enjoyed success alone. Would the image be different, had Matoš headed a Croatian trade mission to Germany, Switzerland, or even France?

"I was born to laugh," he confesses to Ogrizović.[15] "A dead clown after a catastrophe," he tells little Ljerka in his poem. Like Heine, he loved to mock; enjoyed discordancy and change of pace. But laughter, in an otherwise restrained context, can be unseemly and thus destructive. The reader begins to question the author's commitment and sincerity. After all, a politician tells a joke before, not after his dire recital. In Matoš, the imp is at work. The young Andrić observed as early as 1914 that he was, at heart, "a crossroads of dark powers," and went on to say that here the purely joyous child encountered the back-alley criminal; here, a decorous, liturgical silence confronted orgiastic shrieks.[16]

As a personality, then, he left his mark. Indeed, the man is better remembered than the work. Mirko Žeželj sums up: "To contemporaries, he was bohemian, disorderly, superficial, impertinent; a sour and unjust critic, a verbalizer."[17] His own *bon mot*, "de Gustlibus non est disputandum," reads in effect "Let there be but one Gustl" (now and forever).

The critic Gligorić likens "Fresh Cracknels!" to a western movie.[18] He is right. There is a filmic quality which persists from scene to scene and which, despite a bohemian author, rates no parental guidance. Dashing hero bears off fair lady, villain gets comeuppance. The heroine would be well-suited to a John Wayne movie: it takes no effort to visualize a little cabin among the aspens by the river bend where she will live out her days in happiness.

I like to compare Matoš and Federico Fellini (1920–), moviemaker and director of *La Dolce Vita* (1959–1960), *8½* (1963), and *Fellini Satyricon* (1969). True, when Fellini was born, Matoš had long been buried. Yet the two are autistically akin. *8½*, the autobiographical fantasy of a film director, could be Matoš's life script. As he moved time backward, Fellini made of it a private thing. The past becomes self-history or fiction; *Fellini Satyricon* is a sci-fi Petronius.

Under pseudonyms, Matoš's grandfather, parents, and relatives appear in his work; so do members of the Tkalčić family. But he preferred to fictionalize *himself* and was always prepared to give several versions of an escape from Zagreb or an amour in Switzerland or France. He also liked to tell how people liked him.

Both men sensed a public hunger for romance and depravity. Like Matoš, Fellini uses the traveler through time and space—the ubiquitous reporter in *Dolce Vita*, the two boys in *Satyricon*, himself in *8½*. There lay the romance. But, like Matoš, he also suggests the rottenness of the rich and gifted, the commercial attitude of a church which is not even recognizable. In the opening scene of *Dolce Vita*, a statue of Christ is being transported to the Vatican over rooftops where sunbathers in bikinis wonder what it is. Matoš, at most a "cultural" Catholic, attacked the clergy as capitalists. They were stupid and lazy, but held a stranglehold on Croatian life.[19] Teaching orders, such as the Jesuits, bear the brunt of his anger as "the accursed historical enemies . . . of political freedom and free thought."[20] He was appalled that schoolchildren could be expelled for reading Vidrić, the poet, and he bitterly fought the Catholic critic Jovan Hranilović, who preached morality in art.

Critical words like *vrveti* ("to teem") and *zanos* ("inspiration") bespeak the aesthete. Young Matoš brimmed with excitement at a time of sad cello melodies and fading autumn colors. He gives the impression that only a thin line divides waking and dreaming; that a lost childhood lingers within. He promises discovery, but never fulfills the promise. As he aged, the mannerist in him laid down rules for others, while permitting him to reuse themes and routines (such as, the Café Dardanelles invocation) which had proved successful. The critic more and more played favorites. He liked (and pitied) Harambašić. He found the poet Dis proletarian but amusing ("in his company I feel Dis-harmony").[21]

Laughter was his greatest gift, but he never gained a sense of propriety. Perhaps that failure affected his conception of the comic as a departure from the norm ("any disharmony is comic"). Comedy and tragedy were matters of degree: " . . . when disharmony is great, it pains and alarms, and the result is tragedy. When insignificant or small, it makes us laugh."[22] Even that definition, however, did not license malice. It was a lapse to poke fun at Jovan Skerlić's name ("hatmaker's son"); to lampoon an actor's hoarseness (when it was due to illness); to liken Vietnamese music, which he did not understand, to the buzzing of flies and the howling of sick cats.[23]

He plunged into areas where he lacked competence, judging painting and sculpture with the cheeky strategy that he could not go far astray by sticking with the Old Masters. His sensitive piece on K. M. Crnčić owed much to luck. Every literary figure had to be graded. Firdousi was greater than Homer; Darwin, greater than Schopenhauer and Kant. Life seemed to pattern in balanced oppositions and reverse phrases; Plato was a poet-turned-philosopher, while Nietzsche was a philosopher-turned-poet. The notebooks pose questions which are left unanswered.

Questions about himself, for example. One might suppose that his association with art would generate interesting answers as well as interesting questions. Does life validate art? Do aesthetic values sustain one through life's worst crises? If Matoš pondered such matters, he did not record his thoughts. Life pushed him, and he yielded. The struggle for survival never let up. Too often he could not feel enthusiastic about his

subject matter. In addition, there was the mystique with which he surrounded himself—he was the Croat in Serbia, the traveler, the patriot,
Don Juan, the literary Dr. Faustus.

Marijan Matković compares him to a bridge between an older and
a younger generation.[24] During much of his career, he understood Serbia better than Croatia, which he continually misjudged. Politically, he
sympathized with the Starčević rightists, who were nationalists wanting Croatia to stand by herself. But he got caught between them and
the Masaryk pan-Slav liberals of the 1900s, who desired a broad Serbo-
Croatian coalition. He is a classic Mr. In-Between.

Who was Gustav Matoš? When first taking up my pen, I was con-
vinced that his romanticism and laughter put him very much in the
spirit of our era, where old people nostalgically yearn for the past and
young people nihilistically question traditional values. That assessment
still seems valid, even if one more narrowly takes his measure where
literary achievement is concerned. Of course, he deserves the chance
to speak in his own defense, and he might well say aloud what he said
to himself in 1901, jotting down the thought in his notebook: "I am a
clown leaping from the horse of pastness through the hoop of Eternity."[25]

"A Time to Remember" (1900)

But our raised eyes fly
Ah! To where
Each day
The sunlight of our dear homeland breaks.

Petar Preradović (1818–1872)

One serene September evening in 188–, the odd company on the terrace of the Café Kosićeva Vila in Bukovac included Dragutin Hartman, a young physician; the historian and philologist Petrinović; Jelica; and her brother George, a bank clerk, both from town. Before them—wine, roses, vineyards and hills, the woods of Kaptol and Grič: all our glorious Zagreb, its colorful sunlit rooftops fading and sinking into twilight. Further off, still bright, flowed the Sava, silver artery of our Croatian landscape.

A pause ... Then the talk turned to happiness. A crescent moon from beyond the dark forests of Moslavina imparted to young hearts a bittersweet languor. Hearing Zagreb's evening bells in the soft air, the plaint voiced by St. Stephen the King's lion throat and brass clapper, lovely Jelica paled and with a glance at Hartman wiped away a furtive, and probably inexplicable, tear with her sleeve.

Hartman concluded: "So, you see, I was happy only when I believed that happiness did not exist."

"Nonsense! You doctors and priests are pessimists by occupation," volunteered George. "I have always been happy, mainly because I am Zagreb-born. A true native son—not from the new part, but from Kaptol, Gornji grad or Vlaška Street—is every bit as distinctive as a citizen of Paris. Whatever may be argued to the contrary, we are 'the flower of Croatia's spirit and intellect.'"

"And when were *you* happiest?" Jelica asked Petrinović.

Petrinović lit a cigarette. "Be patient. My story is a long one."

I

When I came to Hrastovac the first time, Grga Alagović, a relative of mother's whom we called "uncle," was already the parish priest, having completed his tour as a military chaplain throughout the kingdom. It was his good fortune to escape at Königgrätz. Despite recognition for that heroic deed, he got assigned to the run-down parish of Hrastovac because of a sermon he gave to the border troops. I knew of him only through my father's description. It was said that he refused to acknowledge Hungarian authority; that he avoided trains because of Hungarian conductors; that he was good as bread and sharp as steel; and (unless I am mistaken) that he wrote the music to Antunović's *Kukuriku, viče oroz na zreniku* [Cock-a-doodle-doo, crows the cock for all to see].

In those days I enjoyed fame as a leader of Homeric battles between the classical gymnasium, where I was a student, and the technical school. My Zagreb crowd—with nicknames and titles like Tartalja, Jurica the Trumpeter, Miško, or Žgaga—called me "golden cannoneer" and deferred to me for devising a new pastime: we ate and drank at others' expense and never paid a bill! Once, just at Corpus Christi time, the proprietor of the Golden Cannon confronted us practically in our seats at the gymnasium. (We had been at his establishment the previous night.) I remember, he clutched some chicken bones—they resembled ducats shining yellow in a store window. After that, we kept within the limits of Gornji grad, our "Cannoneer's Kingdom." Unfortunately, there came a time when the cannoneer's parents were advised about all that and told either to withdraw their precious son from school or see him "bounced." Father tossed me into a rustic cart and sternly told the driver, my Uncle Grga's bellringer and sexton: "Šimek, be careful this brat does not escape. I put you on your honor."

My mother, in tears, was visible at a window; and finding a few silver coins she had knotted into a freshly laundered kerchief, I too wept, as if melting into cash. At the Sava Bridge I finally sank, exhausted, into my seat of hay and dozed off.

"Young master, we are here." Šimek nudged me with his whip. He no longer resembled those monsters born when the earth shakes.

Evening . . . A cemetery with thin, twisty crosses. A bullock grazing. A somber church with moss-encrusted shingle roof and two towers resembling minarets. A big green open space fenced with thick poles.

A large linden. Finally, a great old one-story house. The lower part was brick; the upper, frame like those roundabout. On the roof, red metal pennants flew from two peaks. I was aware of stock lowing or ruminating; a drowsy cock crowed. What was that over by the well, a wooden turban with a wooden chicken on top? No, it was a peasant who stared and stiffened. He wore a dirty torn shirt and over his shoulder carried a pig bound in sticks. His toes stuck out of his shoes, and through his ventilated bowler hat there protruded—Oh my God!—a pigtail!

"Andraš, have you slops for my swine?" asked Šimek by way of greeting.

"Yes. By the way, your wife has taken a turn for the worse."

Two lean dogs emerged from the rectory. They snarled and nipped, baring razor-sharp white teeth. I was frightened in my fright-prone Zagreb heart. The cart had stopped before big chained gates, like those of a fortress. The knocker was an iron ring. By the time the portals creaked open, a young cleric (probably a chaplain) had appeared at the door, and as quickly disappeared.

Now, from a hall, I heard a giant's voice: "He's here! Ha, *virga Domini* ["rod of God"], now you are mine!" Dressed in a black kaftan and fez, the giant resembled a shaven but disheveled *hodža* [Muslim priest]. He shied his long pipe at the louder of the two dogs, who howled like a winged snake and with his canine brother made for the garden fence. The Goliath plucked me half-dead from the cart, bore me into the cool, brick-floored room on the left, and set me down on a chair. "Antonija! Time for supper!"

I felt like Odysseus in the presence of Cyclops.

"What's the matter, Zagreb donkey? Nothing to say, no kiss for your uncle's hand?"

The tormentor rumpled my hair, literally blew me into his lap, and began to whisper: "Stop snuffling, Aunt Tončika will hear you. There, there, *virga Domini!*" Uncle Grga wanted only to joke. "Look here! My heart is as soft as your mother's. Wipe your tears. Don't let Tončika see you. Do you know the story of the green sparrow?"

"No, uncle."

"I did *not* say 'No, uncle.' I said: 'Do you know the story of the green sparrow?'" The old tyrant began to roar with laughter, wiping at his tears with a huge blue kerchief. He kissed me. "Oho, *virga, virga,* truly the scourge of God, ho, ho!"

He reeked of smoke and tobacco like a just-emptied café. His left

eyelid remained half-open, making him look distrustful and mischievous. His bluish nose was reminiscent of seaweed or algae; and his
smoke-filled nostrils brought to mind pitch on the bark of a peach tree.
His face was puffy, as though his mouth were full of water; his thick
eyebrows arched like a white vault above a cask in a cellar.

In conversation, he made me look into his eyes—eye, that is—and
had a habit of touching the tip of my nose with his index finger: "That
way, I know whether you're lying!"

At that moment, all in black with black silk shawl, a tall thin woman
entered. She and uncle belonged together, like chapter and verse.
Catching sight of me, she spread her arms, looking like the Greek letter
psi, then raised her eyes like a chicken drinking water and made over
my head the sign of the cross.

"Julček, my child, kiss your Aunt Tončika. I hear, Julček, that they
have done badly by you, as they have by me. But no harm will come
while Aunt Tončika is in charge."

"Yes, Tončika, yes!" Uncle affirmed.

"Poor dear! Don't wait, pitch in and eat. Don't go hungry tonight."

"Your aunt has fixed chicken soup, crêpes with filling, beans and
schnitzel, roast duckling, and strawberries with sour cream because
Rezika said they were your favorites. Tomorrow and the day after, you
won't fare worse. Ever since my father's tannery burned down in Brod,
I know what trouble and injustice are. Ah! Justice is only in God, happiness only in heaven."

While servings of beans flashed past "like a cloud of heavy hail,"
uncle launched into a flowery toast of welcome and passed along a
giant crock of wine. In grateful acknowledgment, I recited snatches of
Latin, Greek, and Croatian (greater and lesser) poetry. I glorified
homeland, uncle, aunt, and chaplain, guzzling a half liter of wine as
though it were a thimbleful, and in the course of my heroics prevailed
upon the chaplain, the Reverend Domogoj Španović, to toast the Croatian people. His humor and his sickly looking head brought to mind
Sterne or poor Yorick. At the duck course, uncle drank to the memory
of his friend, the late Eugene Kvaternik. After a first loving cup, I was
jokingly named director of tables; the chaplain would see that every
glass stayed full; auntie was to be the bouncer. At mention of the
"Alcoholic Statutes of Križevac," Tončika departed. As I drank broth-
erhood with Domogoj and my uncle, barriers fell away like beams
from the ceiling, and I chronicled my final deviltries in Zagreb:

On Jurjevska Street, behind St. George's Church, was the cabin of

Grandpa Petar the milkman and his spindly daughter (nicknamed "Goatgirl" because neighbors frequently saw her with a goat). When I asked for names of new drinking places, Tartalja cleverly suggested that place. We hung around until Petar left with his pails for the city. Inside, I introduced my fellow cannoneers: the moustachioed Tartalja, a tuberculous clerk from Ivanić-Kloštar; likewise, his tuberculous friend, Jurica the Trumpeter. Since both hoped, with the help of God's good air and Zagreb's physicians, to regain lost health, how wonderful if the young gentlemen could spend the night! How easily other matters might be arranged from that point. Our fourth brother, Žgaga *recte* Varalić, who wore pince-nez and an imitation gold chain, was introduced as the brother-in-law of the *ban*. Because he fussed over Goatgirl and patted her fuzzy face, she agreed to our requests and served a marvelous wine from the cellar in an earthen crock. "To the *ban's* brother-in-law!" we toasted, in company with Miss Žuža—for that was Goatgirl's real name. The poor creature, enthralled, watched Tartalja the way a tomcat watches a bishop; while Žgaga, soul of her soul, slipped cigarette ashes into her drink. She became affectionate, then foolish, and after her third glass, drunk as a cork. To our delight, she danced a *czardas* with Žgaga, who limped, while Tartalja shouted encouragement and Jurica played the milkman's accordion. A glass trembled; so did a clock trimmed with ballerinas and bits of colored paper. Feeling no pain, Žgaga and Goatgirl stamped and dug with imaginary hussar spurs. Finally, with a lamp broken and with our *première danseuse* collapsed in a corner, we lit candles, bore Goatgirl by tablecloth to a crypt, and chanted a *Miserere:*

> Let us bury her near the fence,
> So that she does not reach home.

We entered the crypt, i.e., the winecellar. But scarcely had the festival begun when it abruptly ended. Tartalja had just come upon a fresh cask when—there was Grandpa Petar with gun and cane! Prayers, entreaties, tears, self-abasements—nothing would do. The dairyman was not to be appeased. Like Cyclops he led us, one by one, to a hovel by the steep bank of the Tuškanac River, packing us in like sardines, and padlocked the door.

"Yipes! Mother! Something's between my legs! A dog? Ah, there's his ear," somebody whispered. Silence. We tried to group.

"I can't take any more . . . Jesus!" shrieked the *ban's* brother-in-law, as something hit my back and knocked me to the ground.

"Help, Petrinović, help!" groaned Tartalja from the darkness. The tone suggested that he had just been stabbed in the liver. "It was only in fun!"

"O-o-oh!" whined Jurica.

Whatever it was began to plunge around, hitting us on heads and backs, working between our legs; then slashing our stomachs with a dull knife and tossing us from corner to corner. We seemed to be in rinse water, and somebody had a hard sharp tooth.

"It's Satan!" Tartalja's voice was whispery as well as plaintive.

Ow! Two iron fingers poked my ribs, fastened me against the low, vile ceiling, and let me fall like a roundcake, upon my three wretched brothers.

Whump! W-h-u-m-p!

"A billy goat! How stupid we have been! Fellows, take your knives and close in around me. Let's send this hell-hound where he belongs!" I cried.

Silence. We had sobered up in an instant. Our hearts beat furiously. We waited.

"Mother!" Tartalja let out a wail.

The Trumpeter: "Now, cannoneers! Cut out his goatly guts, I'm holding his horns!"

Chaos and confusion! Suddenly everything began to rock. A giant fist was crushing us, like ants in a bag. I grabbed someone's leg. Something hit my head. I saw saints and stars and seemed to be flying in the clouds. Finally I landed beneath a tree on grass. By the full moon, I could plainly see a black avalanche of chicken coop, pigsty, holding pen—whatever it might be!—descending toward a ditch, amid a caterwaul of human and animal voices. All at once, a fellow sufferer came hurtling out. I rushed, that is, slid downhill and collected my friends in the garden. The building hit the ditch like a shot. Another whump! All bloody, our tormentor lay in the brook. The shack had come to rest on his rib. We were about to rescue him when we heard a clomping of boots and a voice: "Wait, you thieves!"

We lit out, scattering into the shrubbery by the Sofija road.

"Stop!"

Bang! went Petar's ancient gun, and Žgaga called in a frightened voice: "I'm hit!"

We brought him home in a taxi before dawn. Dr. Von subsequently diagnosed four pounds of salt (and enough pig bristles to make a brush) in "the organ for sitting." Dairyman Petar narrowly escaped prison, thanks to my father, but here was I in Siberia!

"For such trifles they take poor children out of school?" Aunt Tončika now reentered the room, smiling. She had listened from the kitchen. After a singing of "I am from Varaždin," they led me across a broad hall filled with hedgehog skins and stony columns to what auntie called the *bavlioteka* ["book-browsery"], which henceforth was to be my room. All three saw me to bed. I kissed the hands of my aunt and uncle; they sprinkled my brow with holy water from a bottle above my head among dry catkins, above which was another bottle upon which a skillful beggarly hand had etched a crucifix, a pincers, and other instruments used to torture the Son of God. My roommate the chaplain—my uncle's sickly blue-eyed guest and protegé—silently sat at the foot of my bed, remaining until I closed my eyes. Then he knelt to the etched crucifix, buried his head in his folded clenched hands, and prayed fervently (almost desperately), mostly in whispers, but now and again more loudly. I, too, prayed, but not in words. That night God himself touched my eyelids to sleep.

II

I awoke at dawn and washed and dressed quietly, so as not waken the chaplain, who was breathing heavy and fast, as though in a fever. A lark flew in at the window and perched on a curtain, chirping as if to tell me something. A clock struck, and the frightened bird fled. Cuckoo! It was the little Swiss house on the mantel. On its gates, a clock which showed just 3:30; but a little Capuchin monk, a dwarf as it were, was striking 12:00 with a golden hammer on a golden anvil. The book-browsery was, of course, commodious and full of mousetraps. Besides, it smelled of moths, Styrian eggs, quinces ripening red or yellow in heavy, dark, oak cupboards. In that grey room, my bed shone white, like pigeon eggs in an attic nest. Narrow towels, each long enough to wipe off half the parish, were clean as pebbles in a brook. On the table, atop a thick, bare skin, lay a heap of oppositional-clerical and literary journals, all in Croatian. Also, a glass box from which a young green golden-eyed frog looked out amid yellow sedge, as golden fish swam overhead in unconcern about a peaceful seahog, who rested on the sea floor and rosily dreamed about rush grass and accursed princesses. The entire wall opposite my bed was crowded with cupboards and large folio-sized books, which uncle referred to last night as "lumber room materials."

It was the library of all previous parish priests back to the Tatar invasion. Probably the first book had been brought by King Bela, who (in my uncle's version) overnighted at the marvelous rectory, then granted Hrastovac, jewel of the Turopol Valley, as a personal gift to the *župan* ["tribal leader"] named Vukmanić. Were it not for a German translation of Felix Dupanloup, Preradović's *Prvenci* [The First Born], and volumes from the St. Jerome Society and Matica Hrvatska, I would have believed myself to be in the library of a Ritter-Vitezović or Baltazar Krčelić. For here everything was old, Latin, and Catholic. I was frightened to notice, in one corner, the hellish Voltairean easy chair in which had sprawled the man who plucked proud Hrastovac (as well as other plumage) from the two-headed Austrian eagle. Yes, from the shipboard of this chair, Napoleon threw a sad look and a kiss toward his beloved France. Remembering my own mother and casting a look toward white Zagreb, my Paris and my France, I blew a fresh kiss to the empty Corsican face of my fellow sufferer and fellow exile and sat down to ponder, beside him on the chair: what would be the situation, were Hrastovac today a jewel in the crown of some Napoleon?

A swallow twittered again; above the window were many nests. Underneath, the greyfinger vine twisted among the periwinkle and wafted to my nose, innocently, the welcome cool fragrance of a garden flower still trembling with heavy dew. A rose bent toward a white lily as if to whisper; the lily showed yellow-gold. All the plots ruffled and swayed: lovage, marsh mallow, the silken, divinely green plant we call *plahtica*, even the pink carnation. All murmured and gently moved their colorful lips. Beyond the tree line and the fields of young corn, straw-roofed peasant houses looking like anthills seemed to be wearing heavy winter overcoats. Their dark blue smoke curled into the broad blue heaven.

Whoosh! Somewhere nearby wheels were turning softly. From elsewhere the bleating of stock. A horse in moist clover neighed and leaped clumsily in his hobbles. I could hear mowers' grindstones—a happy sound, like iron quail singing.

Bang! The door slammed. The dark figure of Antonija [Tončika], like a vision, began to pad down the clean yellow path among the rustling foliage and flowers. She was bound for the hornbeam arbor. Passing a buck-naked, stone Cupid who aimed at her an invisible arrow, she crossed herself three times and lowered her gaze. In the courtyard her voice became a bugle.

"Šarl, Šarl!" She made a turn beneath the cherry tree. "Stop teasing the donkey, do you hear? Do you hear, Šarl?"

"Šarl!" a magpie echoed from a large Salzburg pear.

"That is an order!" she added in a deep bass from the courtyard. "Teasing makes you a donkey yourself." She shouted so loud and fast that I could barely catch the words. I rushed to another window and looked out. Šarl, that blockhead from yesterday by the well in his bowler hat, lay in front of the stable, grasping the rear legs of a grey, his big strong arms crossed. It was probably his daily dozen, a way of stimulating his nerve endings. The young animal, tired of being thrown at random, brayed piteously. Finally, the crass Šarl showed mercy, released the donkey, and (as they say in Zagreb) almost flipped him over his ears.

"Easy, easy, Lojzek, you're but a colt." He tried to offer consolation.

Across the way, an old fat servant girl went at a run. A door creaked, and in a flash the broad courtyard was as colorful as the ribs in the roof of St. Mark's in Zagreb. Poultry everywhere, motley and noisy. The proud Crèvecoeur roosters crowed, the small white Turks got wedged underfoot. A progress of Pomeranian and Croatian geese. Tiny chicks around a hen resembled yellow polenta. A flotilla of ducks parted the pondweed with pure silken breasts as they swam beside the trash pile, overgrown with squash. Piglets bolted all around, as from a gun. When Šarl grabbed one by the tail, it began to squeal so frightfully that doves from the cote in mid-courtyard took off like white snowflakes in a wind—in turn causing a stork, who hitherto had rested on one leg like an old invalid, to take flight and hover above the church like a great cross trailing two red bows—his thin legs. An enormous white turkey strutted among its kind like a white moon among pale stars, and above neighboring plum trees the warm summer air floated in sunshine like the turkey's comb. Šarl pinched a fierce shaggy farm dog on the tail, which it began to chase, spinning like the earth on its axis. At the watering trough by the well, the prankster saw to the cattle.

Though I could see that he was not exactly as immaculate as a threshing floor, I ran down to him and we proceeded to the pasture like old friends. Behind the church he extracted from his canvas bag a miserable piece of bacon, offering it to me with filthy hands.

"Thank you, I'm not hungry."

"Eat, eat, you need to grow!"

The poor devil chewed it down himself without any bread. When I told him that he must have a stomach like a duck, he asked me for three old coins. If he swallowed them, could he keep them? I handed over a six-kreutzer and a patagon, which the madman dispatched like pork cracklings! Downing a shot of *rakija* from a flask, he launched more questions. Was it true that God determined battles? Was there only one Black, one Red, and one Dead Sea? What had become of the cock in Zagreb who pulled logs with his beak? Whittling a willow flute, he told me how the citizens of Varaždin had cast him out, condemned him to death and to a grave in the Drava; how at Križevac an ox had been hoisted to the church roof, in hopes of a cure from bloat; how the Stubičanians hunted the Virgin in a woods, because her statue had escaped from their possession; and how some miserable Zagreb cleric saved his bellringer from a woman by stripping naked, rubbing himself with honey, rolling in feathers—and flying to the church steeple. Whenever he paused, his lips remained open, idiotically. He was freckled like a turkey egg and redolent of skunk. He had a nose, and an eye to either side; but only the Devil could say why it sat so strange and bizarre on that pumpkin face. His head resembled a sour cucumber which wanted to be a tomato. Why was his hair so white? One winter's night in the woods near Jamnica he had grabbed a wolf by the ears, and they had looked at each other until dawn.

"Šarl, were you born in France?"

"No. My real name is Andraš. It's only the boss's family call me Šarl. I was born in the church." Thereupon he bent low and picking up a bug from the ground, placed it atop the black surface of his finger. As it flew away, he leaped up in pursuit, crying to the point of a whimper, "see that nice little ladybug!"

The churchbell rang for mass. I returned via the cemetery, taking note of the inscription on one stony cross:

> Muszek dole skerlyak Kayti nasz gespen
> Lustrissimusz SZIEFF ZSUGECZ DE BATINA—BREG tutu jeje.

[Doff your hat, peasant, for here lies the illustrious Štijef Zugec of Batinabreg.]

Around the church ran a low-walled cemetery close, perhaps going back to Avars or Obers, and in it were young plum trees and white geese. The church smelled like a warehouse of old hides; it was bare, orphaned. Evidently, the patron had squandered his substance elsewhere. The white fir boards on the old green pulpit may have owed much to the skillful right hand of Šarl. Since the beheaded figure of St. Anthony of Padua had been consigned to the choir, there remained on the altar only a porcine vestige, a symbol. The church was half whitewashed. Instead of a saint, a spectator saw a strange piece of meat on a martyr's spit; it was being regarded, from beneath the lime, by the hairy phiz of some biblical Jew. In Hrastovac, the whole scene had been reduced to a pair of naked legs sticking out of a bowl. Imagine! A fat, very fat, female hand laid hold of one leg; another hand clutched a knee as if it were Mary Magdalene's hairlock or Hrastovac straw. The entire "heartrending" tableau was being dreamily overviewed by (I think!) a virginal-looking female, her lips pensively locked around her little finger.

Facing the main altar, on the cold sandy stone, a cluster of old pious peasant women knelt on bare knees. On a shaky bench to the right— a patron's section with coats of arms and banners—sat Aunt Tončika, huddled down. She did not notice me in her prayerful zeal. I quickly changed into altarboy's garb and helped Šimek light the candles. The pale, sickly chaplain was also present. He conveyed an impression of "fallen majesty," for after him staggered a ridiculous chicken so tailless that one could see its entire rump. That rump, bald and yellow as it was, brought to mind an elderly tonsured monk. Barely had Šimek expelled the pious poultry when I noticed, across the balustrade, a sentimental bullock eyeing us, the young creature from the cemetery. Trying to suppress a smile, I blurted "et cum spiritu tuo." He gave a bellow, knocked up against the door, and clopped away. Mass over, I stood godfather to the bellringer's child, took breakfast in the garden, and went off with the chaplain to read in the "palace," that is to say, the parish house salon.

In that spacious room one could best understand the hospitality of a venerable family line. Down the middle, from end to end, was a table large enough to provide food and drink for five-fold twelve hungry apostles. On the walls hung pictures of Maria Teresa, Toma Bakač Erdödy, Napoleon III, the bishop of Vrhovac, Baron Franjo Trenk, and members of the current ruling house. Likenesses of Eugene Kvaternik and Ante Starčević were adorned with fresh flowers. According to the chaplain, just the other day my uncle had sent a cask of old Schieler wine to his friend Ante in Zagreb.

Beneath these patriotic portraits lay a guest album which visitors

signed. I found herein an epigram by Stjepan Masnec, may God rest
his wine-loving soul! Also, works by Starčević printed in gold letters;
Kvaternik's *Addresses and Proposals;* photographs of Rakovica village;
and, under glass, a scarf and glove left behind one merry night by
uncle's pupil, Vjekoslav Bach. Then, the photo of a certain P., who
later ran away: on the forehead was written "Bad person!" and on the
jacket a group of signatures, half of them illegible (because of subsequent treachery). At the head of the table an enormous gilded horn,
with the salt of hospitality, along with boot-vases and wine glasses.
Drapes, tablecloths, linen, rafters—in this white room everything was
red, white, and blue. Even Starčević's "God and the Croatians" blazed
in three colors on a door. In one corner stood the standard of Zvonimir,
father of our people. Here, as in all old houses, was a hoard of colored
candles, old Easter eggs, dry pastry, and tricolored braided rugs of
wool or linen; here, too, an all-pervading smell of yellow melons and
red Styrian eggs. What pleased me especially was a two-headed calf
sitting on a cabinet, and a devil who held a candle with his paws and
tail. This devil was large and red and had a long black tongue; because
of him, Šarl would not enter that floor if you promised a banship. The
calf was more clearly dead than alive; it was stuffed and rested among
the parochial *lares* in place of a twin-headed Janus.

No sooner had I begun to read "Hrvatska" ["Croatia"] than my aunt
entered to say, "I have fixed your lunch. What *would* your mother say
if we returned her child hungry and thin?"

I enjoyed the sweet ewe's milk and paprikash stew—so uniquely
good because, that very day, the peppers were still ripening red-hot in
the garden—as I admired the cleanliness of my aunt's room. Butterflies
flitted around flower pots by an open window. Everything was starkly
white: the monastery-type curtains, the bed and its quilt, the white cat
named Fritz who seemed to be lying next to a melting patch of Alpine
snow—auntie's white-white nightcap. Everything was starkly white:
even the socks she had begun for me, and the ivory-bound prayerbook.
All had a bright look, except for my aunt herself, who dressed in black
like an abbess and stood out like an inkblot. And except for the somber
likeness of a knight on the wall, beneath whom (in effacement of an
originally German signature) the firm, puritanical hand of my uncle
had lettered, "Bogomir Bouillon-Soup, the Starčević of the Holy
Grave." Beneath the sad knight, on a shelf, were a spirit-cooker, two
or three large rosaries, a capuchin hood, a dreambook, the famous Šoš-

tar Calendar from Zagreb, and the popular German novel *Peter the Robber, Whip and Shame of the Lika Region.*

Among us a curious saint came to reign. He was tall, with droopy moustaches and cracked wax on his shoes. The green hat in his hand bore a tuft of chamois, and his hair was slicked down as if with butter. He would bend over like a jackknife and bark: "Baron von Fistor . . . er . . . ahem!"; throw himself into a chair, become comfortable, and with a kerchief begin to dab at a pointy nose which resembled the Tower of Pisa. Twisting his head, he looked like a blue-eyed gander warily searching the sky for a hawk. He jammed a finger into his padded vest and wailed: "*Verloren!* All is lost!"

"*Was ist, Heilige Mutter?* Mother of God, what's the matter?" my aunt asked.

While Tončika and Fistor wailed and wept together, the chaplain pulled me to one side and explained, "that is our renowned Turkey Baron from Turopol."

"Please God, what is a turkey baron?"

"Fistor was born in Prussia but raised in Vienna, where he became a postal employee. He also engaged in buying and dressing Croatian turkeys for the large markets."

Consuming his blue tears in a convulsive goulash—and he could eat as if on commission!—von Fistor began his story in loud Viennese dialect. "One evening some ten days ago, a distinguished foreigner came to my office in Hudi Bitek and when we were by ourselves, removed his overcoat. I recognized then, ladies and gentlemen, that I was looking at the unfortunate Sr. X. and fell upon my knees. His was a tragic tale. In effect, because of high-level politics, he was obliged to live secretly for a while. Would I, as a nobleman (a baron who might one day soon be a prince), provide hospitality and help? I swore verily, by my word of honor as an officer of the reserve, that nothing would leak out, so help me God. I would lock him into the salon, personally feed and keep him, and at night let him out into the garden where he liked to walk until dawn in the moonlight.

"Fine. A gracious gesture!" said the chaplain.

"Ach, ja!" wailed the Turkey Baron. "Fine for you. Two mornings ago, I went at dawn to find him, to lift him back through the window. But nothing! He was not in the garden, the meadow, the mill; it was as if the estate had swallowed him up. Since no village or settlement lies nearby, no further information was available. What if the wretch had drowned in the Lomnica? What if evildoers had done him harm? Like a madman I went to the bridal chamber of Baroness Fistor, née Klappermaul zu Habichtshausen—only to find it empty! All that remained was my dachshund crouching under a bed and howling piteously! I looked elsewhere under beds and in cabinets. Nothing!"

"Besides your wife, did the swindler take your turkey money?" asked the chaplain.

"Yes, *Hochwürden*, Your Reverence."

"But why did you not bring charges, send telegrams around? What have you been doing all these past two days?"

"Who can act or think when his wife is with another? It's too late now! The deceiver may already be in Italy or at sea."

I left the tearful baron and went with the chaplain to the garden. The temperature was stifling. A fat thrush, made stupid by the heat, lolled on a branch.

I espied currant lushes, some coral-red, others yellow, like strings of pearls. A mole crossed the hard yellow path and drilled his pink snout into the ground.

"Psst!" the chaplain whispered. He entered the shrubbery. I followed, munching berries. We squatted down.

Before us in the grass, beneath an appletree, lay a young girl weaving field flowers into a daisy chain. She hummed and plucked, plucked and hummed so gently that, undisturbed, a spider descended his silvery thread toward her legs and a golden emerald beetle passed by into the green grass. After the strange girl—fairy, nymph, or whatever—had finished with the yellow and white flowerheads, she picked up a poppy well past its bloom and began to hum anew, in monotone with the bees around her locks: "Black mare, white stallion / White mare, black stallion. . . ." Her face hidden behind a broad straw hat, her tresses edged in gold hanging down to her narrow shoulders, she lay sideways. I could barely see her dark neck (on which she wore a simple blue necklace). She had sallow, thin, supple hands and deerlike, gypsy-brown bare legs.

The chaplain identified her as Smiljka, daughter of an eccentric schoolteacher in the village. Her father gave organ lessons at the church, and she herself was so talented that just last winter she had played at all the pre-Christmas sunrise services. She sang like a cherub and not a day passed without her going to practice afternoons in the church. But this spring, at Easter, she fell asleep there, while awaiting the young rascal who worked the bellows. Her father, a widower, was off somewhere, and the maid Dora wrongly assumed that the child was at the parish hall, and Šimek locked up earlier than usual. Next day, they found her in a heap beneath the eternal flame—she had gone mad.

A shadow played on a mossy stump, a blackbird sang—also, a wild dove and cricket. Smiljka hummed: "The King of Heaven is born to us. . . ." Then suddenly she took fright, listened, and began to call: "Countess! Countess!"

A frightful racket began in the trees, and a crow descended upon her back, shrieking wildly and beating its wings. She still did not see us, lurking like thieves just opposite. "Ah, God, how pretty!" I sighed. Her large opal eyes drew me the way orchids draw flies, her features were such as had appeared only in my feverish innermost dreams. So, I emerged from the shrubbery, only to see her break into a run. I gave chase, losing my cap in the thick clover. When finally I caught her, she began to pull my hair. The feeling was good and I sang: "Black dove, white blackbird / White dove, black blackbird. . . ."

She responded: "They're getting uncle up, / 'Cause Mama's fixing rabbit." Her voice sounded tearful; I hoped not entirely on my account. She smiled with pale soft lips and white gypsy teeth. I kissed her clumsily—on that eye of a mother or a flower.

"Might you be *ban* or bishop?" she stabbed her sharp, shaky elbows into my chest. "If a *ban*, hold me. If a bishop, let me go!"

"I am a *ban*, and you my wife!"

We laughed. My heart surged like a young colt, and we took off through cornfields, undergrowth, and brambles, until her white cheeks fairly exploded with blood and our arms and legs were exhausted.

"Yes," she said, slumping down beside me, "you're truly a *ban*." Humming she plucked my hair and chewed grass. I softly kissed her moist tresses.

When Andraš arrived with his cows and his flute, she fell asleep in my lap. Stealthily touching her breast, I translated into my young and passionate veins the violent pounding of her mad heart. Far off in ruins lay medieval Okić and Susjed (homeland of Petrica Kerempuh and the evil Franjo Tahi) and like a woman prodding forward her petrified child, walled Medvedgrad on the side of Zagreb Mountain. Would this mad sister awaken and lead me beyond the slopes of Vukomerica and Kupa, to the massif of Klek, that legendary resting place of Kraljević Marko, where other white vilas consorted with the temperamental Grabancijaš, their disciple? Šarl tucked the flute into his belt, swatted at flies with a birch twig, and told me about the Black Queen and the Snake King, as if discussing some official and his wife.

The sun got behind the wooded hills of Žumbera, the sounds of Angelus faded. In fact, the sky was aglitter when I brought my own pale star into the silent parish house. Aunt Tončika offered her snowy-white bed. From the garden, the sounds of guests . . . I could distinguish "O Tannenbaum" as sung by the Turkey Baron. Exhausted, I withdrew to the book-browsery, for the Sandman was nigh. I heard my aunt praying next door, her words like the clucks of a setting hen.

III

The chaplain awakened me at dawn with news of Baron Fistor's death only hours earlier. Yesterday he had wagered to eat a cooked chicken, bones and all. The chaplain, strong-willed as Hamlet, put together some melancholy thoughts.

"What is human life?"

"What day is today, sir?"

He smiled bittersweetly and retorted, "Friday, the Turkish holy day."

"You seem to have got up on the wrong side of the bed."

"Neither right nor wrong. I spent all night in the garden waiting for the rabbit who has been stealing our fruit. I've no hunting license, that's true. But what has the world come to if one cannot defend oneself from a wolf or kill a predator without a license?"

"True. Where's the rabbit?"

Again the bittersweet smile. The chaplain reached into his sack and extracted the white (starkly white) corpse of Fritz the tomcat, beloved of Aunt Tončika.

"A really unlucky day," I said sympathetically.

Only after getting dressed did I think of Smiljka. Yesterday seemed a dream—until I heard tamburitzalike sounds and ran to my aunt's chamber. There was Smiljka at a clavichord which just yesterday I had taken for an antediluvian table. While she played, my aunt curled her hair and said: "Fine! Now we'll put on the silk stockings and the slippers which Dora has brought. Stay as good as now, child, and I shall see that you marry Julček."

"The *ban*?"

"The *ban*, the *ban*, my chick, my dove!"

Leaving my keyhole post, I joined Šimek downstairs. It was time to ring the bells. How I feared that my heartbeats could be seen through my vest! From the direction of the cemetery came howls and shouts, the sounds of a struggle and of someone being choked, perhaps killed. What a sight! A giant was sprawled on the grass, shrieking like a hog at slaughter. With two hands, he held two peasants by the stomach and was shaking them the way he had shaken the donkey's legs a couple of days ago. He seemed to be in convulsion.

A dwarf-sized Hector was pulling all three bodies around the walls of Troy, while berating Andraš: "Easy there, this way, Herr von Čuč-nik. It's got to come out, you dog's leg. Whew!" His exertions made him look lumpy, like a blood sausage, and his red face might have been the Bloody Bridge between Kaptol and Grič in the fourteenth century, at the time of Gordun of Gorica. He was sweaty and as wet as the Sava at flood-tide. "Now there, *ruhig*, Andraš, alias Šarl de Ču-u-u-čnik. Grab him, the wretch, and hold on! It's got to come o-o-u-u-t-t!" cried the little fellow, continuing to drag and torment his victim. When the human pileup had worked its way from the first church tower to the second, martyr Andraš-Šarl von Čučnik emitted a wail so heartrending that a cat nearby, from the cemetery, took flight with a yowl, crashing into the three-cornered stone hat of Saint Ivan Nepomuk [ca. 1330–1390] on the church wall. In a kind of ecstasy, it meowed loud and clear.

"Lord Čučnik, your noble tooth is out!" shouted the rosy tyrant. He rolled on his back. From his forehead a household cap sailed across the fence to the wooden cross on a gravesite. From his pocket something white and large emerged, which I took for a cosmetic box but which proved to be a watch. At that moment, Andraš bellowed as if wounded. He fastened one peasant against a wall, and nearly hurled the second through the church door. Then the martyr rinsed his mouth from a bucket brought by another Turopol nobleman, a spectator like us.

I accompanied Šimek to the belfry. His bell was called the Fat Virgin; mine, less heavy, was the Zinker or Death Bell *(Cinkuš)*. How beautifully they went together! Coming out, I espied our glorious barber lolling under a plum tree and—it was hard to believe my eyes—sticking out his tongue!

By way of explanation, he said: "In truth sir, nothing natural is shameful, *naturalia non sunt turpia*. Let young people in school know our feeling that only a natural state can provide man with a happy life. I act like a dog, just like a Vlach, I mean, a Greek. A dog enjoys healthy lungs because he sticks out his tongue when he feels hot. I am your humble servant *(servus humillimus)*, young master. Be so kind as to remember me to your uncle and tell him that we shall be over in another week to let his blood. Let him, as a priest, steer clear of doctors, remembering: *timeo Danaos* ("I fear Greeks . . .")."

After a citizen of Hrastovac named Drmačić disappeared on a dusty road near some isolated peasant homes, I learned from the sexton that the barber was in reality Ciprijan Golubić, an aristocrat and former "blackbird" or theological student. He could put a devil on your back or determine the outcome of a local quarrel, like an Orthodox priest. My uncle esteemed the fellow, even though he never attended church.

It was Sunday, "God's day of rest," as the poet says. By and by, the church and environs became colorful with peasant coats, shirts, ornamental dresses and kerchiefs—like a meadow of flowers. Šimek and I served at uncle's mass. From a corner Aunt Tončika observed me with beneficent eyes; next to her, the chaplain buried his pale head behind thin, clenched hands. I was affected by the incense and organ music; the congregational hymns (so solid and tuneful and pious); the antiphonal contrast between my uncle's rough voice and the schoolteacher's splendid baritone. Aunt Tončika said later that she had never heard him preach better. At one point during the sermon, my eyes and nose prickled as I was addressed by an old widow, wrapped in a blanket and blue kerchief. She sighed loudly, "Jojček, you darling!" Her further wailing was picked up by half of Hrastovac, including my fellow server Šimek.

After mass I came upon the schoolmaster Jelić in the sacristy. His face reminded me strongly of an Aesculapius next to the window of a Zagreb drugstore. Pale, laconic, with a whispery voice, he was a proper widower. Thanking me for rescuing Smiljka yesterday, he said that I had the makings of a physician to the mad, and that he did not envy me the gift. A congenial type. Not long after, I was invited to his home.

The school (part of it the schoolmaster's quarters) adjoined a stable with two cows, enormous stanchions, and a basement. It was a long, one-story structure, without a chimney. From what purported to be a kitchen, smoke issued from a crude rustic fireplace and trailed out to a frame porch with virtually unhewn columns beneath an old blackshingle roof. In its course, it licked with soft blue tongue at the grey windows of room and school, which were patched with sooty, yellow parchmentlike paper. I marveled at the garden and greenhouse. There were a hundred kinds of roses: yellow (suggesting death), cloud-pink, bleeding-heart red; and calamint past counting. A pear tree with fruit looked like a candlestick which the teacher had done up for Christmas. Other fruit trees had been wired to increase their yield; one had three different varieties. A vineyard of California and Bordeaux grapes grew behind the house. Beyond a green hedge, bees buzzed in golden array. Their hives contained movable honeycombs of the Dzierzon type. Indeed, I had never seen so many Dzierzon hives in one spot.

Jelić spoke only in phrases and half-utterances. In mid-sentence he might break off with "et cetera" or "and so forth," pause and look off into space, shake his head and carry on within himself. Yet in the space of fifteen minutes he had touched upon the current acquisitive spirit in Croatia; the sad fact that many of his friends were spies; and his work, which was onerous and underpaid.

J. E. Tomić had just come out with his *Anecdotes*. Jelić considered him unjust for ridiculing a class which had given the homeland a Fili-pović, a Fabković, a Modec, and a Trstenjak, among other budding, zealous workers. "Whom the Gods hate, they make into a schoolmaster," he added.

"Do you smoke?" His tremulous, elegant hand proffered an expensive tobacco, strong as poison. He chain-smoked. We sat down beneath a spreading ancient cherry. Old Dora the servant brought fresh warm milk, corn-based sweet rolls with butter, and golden, almost transparent, hive honey. I had barely launched into politics when the teacher, who appeared to be dreaming, pursed his lips, raised a finger into the air, and cut me short: "Listen!"

I strained my ears. Nothing. Nothing at all. He half-closed his eyes, stared up into the leaves, and began to whistle in long measures: "Fee-fee-fee. . . ." I could see only a stag beetle beating its wings. "Aha! There he is! The very *Schwartzplättchen* ("black-cap") I've been hunting all month. The female must be near by." In a jiffy he spread a green net, purchased from Hagenauer's in Zagreb, in a clearing beside the tree and set out bait. Then, in a frenzy of excitement he retreated to the porch on tip-toe so as to observe the results.

I made my way into the low, narrow schoolroom, where the sounds of a great subterranean orchestra reached my ears. Through a door I was greeted by: tsrrr! fee—fee—fee! tsee-tsee-goo! tsee-yoo, tsee-yoo! tsoo-kit! tsoo-kit! More than thirty cages occupied the floor and walls, right up to the ceiling. In that colony or moist prison surely every Mid-dle-European bird must have been represented: our blackbird, gold-finch, wren, blind lark; the noisy Danubian *Sprosser* [nightingale]; adorable chattering canaries from an aviary in Hartz. My brain boggled, my ears threatened to burst. Outside, neither net nor teacher were to be seen.

Something landed on my back. Quivery tentacles applied unequal pressure to my neck and eyes. I turned, recognizing those thin little hands yet not daring to kiss them.

"You are *not* a *ban*, but a student," cried Smiljka, blushing.

We clasped hands and went off to the hayfield. There, in some shrubbery, was Jelić, who did not see us, his gaze being fixed upon a *cerrus parva* in the branches overhead. Smiljka seemed too beautiful to be admired directly. I got pleasure just being where she walked. In a shady spot she asked me to help remove her slippers, lest they get dirty. I had thoughts of running away, but kept my calm. Smiljka sang a few country songs.

Again I carried her home. For some reason I felt ashamed, and though our fat cook Slovenka brought in the evening meal I had no appetite.

What a sight greeted my dull gaze through the window! From the Zagreb road a coach trolled up in a cloud of dust. It contained the fat, top-hatted P., our national representative, as well as Miss N., his actress-companion. Out from the garden, thronged with guests, Uncle Grga came at a run to greet them. Miss N. was waving her red parasol in anticipation when suddenly Top-hat let forth an ungodly shriek: uncle's bull had broken from the stable! Head lowered, nostrils dilated like a winged snake and breathing hard, he was headed for the parasol. The representative and his lady lost no time in re-entering the coach while Uncle Grga ran around throwing stones, waving a blue kerchief and yelling, "get him, Andraš-Šarl, this ox of God, this crocodile . . . !"

The mighty Andraš-Šarl, pitchfork in hand, materialized atop a dungheap—Poseidon riding the dark waves—shouting, "back, Dečko, back, boy, back!" But alas, the aforesaid bull was in no mood for appeasement. Inserting his powerful neck between the two rear wheels, he hoisted the carriage on its two front ones while from within two desperate cries were heard, cries quite nonpolitical and nondramatic. Into the air rose the driver, like a chicken out of a fire. On the way down he grabbed for the horses' tails and they, poor creatures, took off as if pursued by vilas. Andraš hooked into the bull's bridle but it was "the Lord of Čučnik" who was now hoisted like a bale of hay by Dečko's short, powerful horns. And he came down to earth square upon his "sitting organ." The ground shook. Goosedown and white duck feathers filled the air.

The people's representative and the actress were seen no more at the parish house.

I continued to feel ill-disposed and sad.

"What is it, my treasure?"

"Nothing."

"Auntie's little mischief-maker has fallen in love."

"How is Smiljka?" I whispered.

"In my room, murmuring your name in her sleep."

For a long time I lay awake. The cock had crowed three times before I shut the window. To no avail. It was dawn before sleep finally came. By then I had composed a tearful letter home, to mother. It included this first, and last, attempt at a poem:

Hrastovac Nocturne

Dear mother, how can I begin
To tell you of my sickness unto death?
My golden-haired Smiljka,
She is my sickness.
Dawn. I cannot sleep.
Dark thoughts like bees follow me through the house,
While a cock cries at the gate:
Sleep, sleep, Smiljka my chick!

IV

Time flies like a greyhound. Mornings I would awaken uncle by pinching his nose—he responded to nothing else! I rang the bells, served at mass, fed the chickens and sacked up pigeons, or the bats which hung like dark hams from the church loft rafters. I took walks with Smiljka, who seemed more rational every day. After lunch the chaplain would tutor me in the garden for one examination or another. Or I might read Freudenreich's *Udmanić* to Smiljka in the deserted park of old Hrastovac, or collect shells and flowers, or row on the ancient estate pond full of turtles and carp. More than once I visited the barber, always managing to discover two or three noodles in his goatish beard. I helped the teacher at school. With my uncle and the chaplain I paid visits to aristocratic Turovo polje and to Pokuplje, the sad heart of sad Croatia. I marveled at the ruins of Samobor, Okić and glorious Ožalj-grad, saw wonderful Mokrice and old Slavetić, seat of the venerable Oršić line. I quickly grew accustomed to an old fowling piece, although the first time I killed a prize calf instead of a sparrow and nearly dislocated a shoulder because of the powerful recoil.

Among our frequent visitors Count B. was reputed to be the most silent member of the Croatian, or any other, parliament. He would arrive daily, precisely at ten, rain or shine, to nip appreciatively at uncle's brandy and to broil himself until afternoon. He was usually alone, and I cannot recall his ever speaking in a normal tone. Instead, he whispered, as though suffering from a sore throat. Since his face was permanently florid as if rubbed with Easter-egg dye, his moustaches and hair yellow like oakum; I found it hard to believe that this mute with the ever-present topper and silk jabot had only ten years before been accounted one of the Dual Monarchy's most formidable warriors, a hunter of women and foxes, a high-roller at the tables. Once only did he make a gesture toward audibility. It was when the discussion concerned rich old Baroness Bonati's purchase of a Slavonian estate for her lover, the young and handsome Count Željesković. At this *our* count leaped up, waved his arm like a saber, opened his lips as if to speak and then, collapsing back, he whispered, "ah, villainy!"

Another constant visitor was Captain Vurdelja, a retiree who enjoyed a strange diversion. He attended every hanging in our happy land, keeping a chronicle from which he would read. I came to believe that every Croat died heroically, even on the rope of shame. Vurdelja must have told me a hundred times how the Border Guards brought flatirons back from Vienna, thinking them to be made of gold.

We loved to set each other silly riddles. He would say, for example, "a hunchbacked pig grazes all over a field. What is it?"

"A lawyer!" I would reply and the captain would burst out laughing and call me a scamp, which made me break all out in prickles.

Another guest, the one-armed Baron Radovan Bojković, who had spent the winter in Paris, I would see only by night. (He was the son of Mrs. Piljević, who could tell you at precisely what hour of the afternoon every "fine Zagreb lady" took *café au lait*.) When Bojković lost his job as collector of the Zagreb retail tax he left Hrastovac to work as estate foreman for a certain Medeković, who had made a good buy on the property of a certain nobleman in J. Rado might be accounted the greatest liar in Croatia were it not for an artist in Zagreb who feigned epileptic lameness and who adored flowers, lies, and music.

The single unpleasant specimen was old Dr. Mauruš from Zagreb. He seemed not to breathe, and he moved his head like a crocodile, shaking it and looking at you crookedly from under his brows. Because he preferred to wear dark glasses well below his eyes and also favored a black nose patch, from afar he resembled a death's head. His wife had a face whose left side was fiery red. She always bore some sad tale to my aunt about the insolence of serving girls to her husband. One had addressed him familiarly while wearing a chapeau! Mauruš himself spoke exclusively of his son, Emil, a student in Vienna. It was Emil this and Emil that. Invariably he would interject: "On a trip to Vienna a man asked why I traveled in third class while my son always traveled in first. I replied that had I a rich father like Emil's I, too, would go first class. . . ."

Before bedtime I read the papers to uncle, and when he felt unwell (which happened about every evening) he would lie prone for a rub. I trampled all over his corpulent, cabbagelike back until he cried out "hey, not so rough! . . . ah, that's good . . . oof! *virga Domini!*"

During these leisure hours he talked about travels in Italy, Austria, and Germany. In later days he had abandoned travel, not wishing to enrich the Hungarian railways. In my uncle's house only Croatian (i.e., Bosno-Hercegovinian) tobacco was smoked. No family in the land supported without stint more causes like the medical faculty, the Croatian theater, the various national charities. For hours he would expound upon local politics.

Once some musicians came from Samobor, a lame barrel-organ player and his squinty old wife. They fell to fighting and in trying to separate them I felt blows on my own back. The man had leaned on a trough, unscrewed his wooden leg and thus defended his one-eyed wife! Only moments earlier Uncle Grga had observed, "these people, *virga Domini,* are more decent than our Catholics and Orthodox."

With considerable scholarship he could tell you which city was nobler: royal Križevac or arch-ducal Karlovac. He regarded the Varaždin Guards as the yeast from which another Svačić might prepare a new and free Croatian loaf. Upon the fall of Napoleon III, he "rolled his tired eyes," like a Petar Zrinski or an Ante Starčević, in the direction of a sultan or subking. In knowledge of foreign politics he matched any minister and was well acquainted with major European statesmen. Once he shamed me in public. Barely had I mentioned "*Glédstin*" and "*Róshfor,*" when quickly laying a hand on my shoulder and a magisterial finger on my lips, he said, "all very well, *virga Domini,* but the names are *Glád-stone* and *Roche-fórt.*" Everyone snickered at my expense. Again, it was the mode in those days for students to translate Heine. I read my own translation to a luncheon group of district clergy, without mentioning the author's name. All were pleased but Uncle Grga, who tapped me on the shoulder and said: "the German version reads, I think: 'Spuckt im Gemüthe' ['spits in emotion'] and should have been rendered *'Pljuje u čuvstvu'* or *'Pljucka u čuvstvu.'"* Was he teasing? I do not know.

Uncle enjoyed forcing his guests to drink. His was an eternal opposition, based on principle. Compassionate and prone to tears like a schoolgirl, he was also rash and quick to explode like a mortar shell. He especially disliked Jews and fleas. Once, wailing and huffing, he knocked me to the ground when I had, ever so gently, landed on his meaty back:

"Ha, *virga!* Jump, hunt, grab, beat!"

"Uncle, what in the world . . . ?"

"Beat! Grab! Hunt! Jump! Don't you see?"

A large flea leaped from my uncle to the prayerbook. Grumbling as he did when his tie would not tie, he broke the glass on his watch. The flea jumped from prayerbook to floor. Boom! A pound of lead from his old gun spilled the metal bowels of the easy chair. What suffered the most during these excesses was the pipe which he carried day and night and which he (voluntarily) yielded only at the sacristy door. A cross on the bowl, embellishing the forehead of a yellow monster, big as a fist, had been badly twisted.

Once we had taken up the church tax and were waiting for some Zagreb students to return with plain green wreaths for a grave. Behind us on tiptoe came the chicken with the bald derrière, bearing in her beak a large entrail from the house. A duck supervened to snatch the booty, whereupon a gander robbed the duck, and a turkey, the gander. But up flew a cock, the most splendidly bannered and spurred of all, and grabbed both the piece of gut and the turkey's fleshy comb. The feathered flock moved off in anticipation of a fray. I left my bench and headed for a lime tree behind which nature's noblemen would likely escape uncle's disapproving glance. One step. Two. Then uncle shouted after me. The whole group, militants and pacifists alike, scattered, leaving the internecine entrail in the grass.

"Oooh . . . God! . . . *Virga!* . . . *Pix infernalis* ["Pitch of Hell"]!"

He was lying on the ground. My moving off the bench had upset the balance.

"Well! Do not look so strange, *virga infernalis!*" Spitting out turf, my uncle sprang up heroically like a cork from a bottle, and collected his dreadful pipe in one hand and his cape in the other. Woe to me!

"Grab the sinner, stop him!" he exhorted the bellringer who was laughing in his beard and who, fortunately, had an armful of flowers and bottles. Three times, like Vukašin after Marko Kraljević, uncle pursued me around the church; even today I cannot explain how I got to the soft lap of my aunt. She locked behind me the door of her snow-white room. There, someone else's embrace effaced furious Uncle Grga.

"Neither a ban *nor* a student, just my beloved. . . ."

"Kiss her, young fool!" urged my aunt. "If she is obedient and good, she will become your wife."

My heart was in my mouth. As I kissed her cool pale lips, I was aware through the window of red centifolia in the garden below. My aunt reddened. The snowy room, too, was turning red.

From below, a rousing song and tamburitza music: students! I stayed with Smiljka. But on my way back from the schoolhouse that evening, I saw a light in the tower and found there a strange company, packed in like sardines.

"Aha! The nephew of the priest, the well-known black sheep of Zagreb!" I recognized the soft voice of Alojzije Strižić from Dubrovnik: a red Boka Kotor cap on his head, a tricolored sash at his trim waist, a peasant jacket over his broad shoulders. So *he* was singing this spring with frogs and nightingales!

They greeted me by turns with wine-flavored kisses or extravagant introductions. The university elite! Here was crook-nosed Rapalić, with the shortest hair and longest tongue of any Croatian writer ("shortest" because he was bald); the heroic Aufzac of Karlovac, with his crippled, twisted right hand, "the provocateur," "bane of the authorities," our "toothpick legs." A real lady's man. "We'll meet at Filip's . . . no, at his lady friend's, I mean at Pepica's."

Here were Pepe Kokotbreg from the Lika, and taciturn Nikola Hegedušević, the patrician of Osijek and the dread of Zagreb's sinister "polyp-panders" ["spies and police"]. Pepić Broz was on hand from Zagorac. He saw himself as a second Stanko Vraz, consumed alcohol solely from two-liter containers and after a third drink, would swallow a button on a string, only to draw it back up and resume drinking with doubled zeal. He, too, was a poet, but (unlike others) wrote only in the absence of inspiration. Celebrities were as thick as towels in a rich peasant dowry.

At a window stood a tall willowy youth with blue eyes and dense blond moustache. My heart thumped: it was my first sight of the famous poet Gusta Hajdukić from Slavonia, the man for whom young Croatian girls sighed at night, the favorite of our late Starčević.

"*Silentium!*"

"Gentlemen, brothers, friends!" The voice from the window was mellow.

"Let him speak! Long live August, Gusta! Silence!"

The poet's head and shoulders were silhouetted against the silken evening sky. I listened, breathless, to his words.

"Brothers, look out these narrow windows. See how this magical landscape glows in the setting sun, like the king's bloody vest in Gora Petrova. It shines serenely like the crown of Tomislav; darkens like the glory of Krst Frankopan; fades into twilight like the glory of our fathers. Look there at Šenoa's white Zagreb nestling beneath its mountain, a hero's eye beneath a helmet. Behold the ruins on the hillsides, stony skeletons of our history and heroism; the huts of our brother peasants; our parishes and aristocratic dominions; our forests, fields, and mountains. All that is our cradle, our patrimony, our homeland. It far exceeds this time and place. Croatia out there beckons. Wrapped in her dim evening robe, she is the greater because, like us, she is both sad of heart and large of soul. Behold, night means the advent of foreigners and traitors. Our night will be dark, like the graves of victims and heroes and nameless patriots sleeping in thin border furrows. Brothers! Friends! Let us be torches and candles in the darkness, clarions to the multitudes dreaming a last sleep. Friends and brothers! With love for our cradle and our grave, let us be Croatian!"

"Hear, hear! Ring Virgin and Zinker!"

"Swear to it, lads!" From below, Uncle's head emerged on a ladder. "Swear by this old silver cross, and damnation take him who swears untrue!"

Tears welled up in me and sweet icy jets whipped my blood. Weeping like a child I put my hand on the cross and joined the others: "I pledge my word, as Christian and Croat!"

Then, after blind pale Bradić of the stolid peasant brow was done, I grabbed the rope of Zinker, while others swung the Fat Virgin, and on coppery wings, my uncle's prayers and the students' tearful hopes went forth:

> Clear and bright in memory,
> Our Croatian anthem flies
> Over the valleys and beyond the hills. . . .

Two days later I would learn from the newspapers that Aufzac and Hegedušević had been wounded and the others arrested beneath the broken windows of a Croatian politician's home.

V

I was just sitting under the lime tree with my aunt. . . .

"Your servant, golden cannoneer!" Varalić embraced me, glorious Žgaga, husband-not-to-be of Miss Goatgirl from Veleslav and fellow sufferer from Goattown (our name for the dairyman's place of torture). With him was an idler, a wandering player and orator named Toša Ujnin (Brother Theodore), who had encountered lame Žgaga in Nova Gradiška and abandoned the laurel groves of the Protić Society to go on foot from village to village, from priest to Orthodox priest. Toša wore patent-leather shoes and a Šumadija jacket. Around his neck, a Byronic kerchief; his headpiece more umbrella than hat. Both men were hirsute, swarthy, looking the part of robbers. They perspired and smoked like steam baths.

Toša introduced himself to my uncle as "a poor starling, a church mouse." At Glina, a pickpocket had approached, but Toša warned him: "Get away, you imbecile, or I'll take your last stolen penny!" An old woman near Bjelovar prophecied a brilliant future for Žgaga, "the *ban's* brother-in-law." "It contained some curious details," said Toša, bringing a drumstick to his eager lips. "But if Balaam received a prophecy from an ass, why not Žgaga from a hag?—if you'll forgive the word."

"Are you a Vlach?" Uncle opened his eyes wide and made a semi-circle with his pipe stem.

"No, sir, an Orthodox Croat from Belgrade," replied Brother Theodore, taking the drumstick with his teeth in the Orthodox manner. An insane smile came over me when I noticed how like the good-natured Lojzek he was, that late bellringer of St. Mark's, whose portrait hung to the left of the choir.

Žgaga described how a three-day storm had overtaken them outside Vinkovci. Lacking money, they approached a tavern "to obtain credit." Entering the courtyard, Toša used his walking stick to kill two or three roosters for paprikash stew. He assumed the role of an English doctor modeled upon Phileas Fogg. *Ikavski*-speakers, gypsies, and bagpipers all in one, they prevailed on the tavern keeper to advance money, presumably for a wire home. The storm passed, fifty florins' worth; but the two priests (one Orthodox, the other Croatian-Catholic) were not yet prepared to give in. As luck would have it, the proprietor took sick and summoned Toša. The young English doctor diagnosed a serious case of gastritis. Since no drug store was present in P., the brothers betook themselves by speedy Slavonian coach to Vinkovci, where Žgaga compounded honey, sugar, lard, yogurt, and pepper. The haughty Briton disdained even a pence of compensation. Astonished, the proprietor's wife kissed the right hand of this virtuous gentleman and begged the kindness of a photograph when they reached "fair England."

By next morning they were in the vicinity of Jastrebarski. "Go, Jajnko! Hey, Jurek, look what a mare that yokel is driving! Giddyap, Štijef!" Toša, Žgaga, and their benefactor the druggist flew out of a tavern and saved the life of a Zagreb cyclist, the first ever seen in that village.

Aunt Tončika did not buy their story in every detail. "Is it true that in Serbia poor women must wash the feet of guests?" she asked Toša.

"True. Our women wash people's feet. But in your Vienna, Budapest, and Zagreb they wash other things as well."

"How's that?" Uncle exploded, twisting his pipe-stem to a thirty-five degree angle.

"Yes, Your Reverence, shirts and other equipment." The impecunious starling calmly prepared to fill his mouth with biscuits and pork cracklings.

Aunt Tončika hurried out, blushing. Uncle Grga bit his lower lip.

In the evening the chaplain departed for Gleichenberg, where tragedy had struck an entire household. Uncle was in tears.

I could not sleep because of the odd juvenile fright that a witch sat atop my chest. Even though awake, I dared not call for help, and finally dozed off only at dawn.

A terrible yell, followed by pounding at my door! Fortunately, uncle came to open it, and into the room burst our fat old cook, howling like a hyena on a Turkish grave. Her negligée was so immodest that uncle turned his broad back.

"What is the matter?"

"Downstairs, sir, outside the window. . . ."

Uncle went for his gun, as I followed. Outside the dark kitchen window I glimpsed a skull, whose moans sounded like a childish duet. Flames were shooting out of the mouth and eyes.

"Swounds!" thundered uncle. He looked pale.

"The Unseen One!" wailed my aunt from behind. A coldness overspread my back and head, when pow! went the gun, and the skull fell apart. Instant two-part lamentations could then be heard beneath the window.

We ran out and in the dungheap by the pitchfork of Andraš von Čučnik discovered none other than Toša and Žgaga—the one wearing uncle's slippers, which resembled children's coffins, the other (the "*ban's* brother-in-law") wearing uncle's sack pants. They had laid upon these parish-house goods as keepsakes. Yet before going on their weary way, they had constructed this monstrosity, made from rags and with a church candle inside, for a bit of entertainment at the expense of a pious and godfearing old servant.

Now the disappearance of uncle's long-lived pipe can be explained: for stem and top both sailed out, bouncing off Toša's hellish backside into a swamp.

I slept until supper.

When I went to find Smiljka, a dark bird of omen confronted me. Jelić said tersely that she had gone with his friend the doctor to Ogulin. Smiljka's soul was lily-like and missing that sweet aroma now, I felt near death. The schoolhouse roses became bloody wounds; dead, faded eyes. I left and finding myself alone in the darkness, I chewed grass like a sick dog. Then I made off across fields and pastures toward Smiljka, in the direction of Karlovac.

They found me at dawn—pale, collapsed, and wet with dew—on a section of track between Leskovac and Jaska. My head rang as if to split. Had a train passed in the night? I could not say. My lungs were inflamed.

VI

God gives us what we can bear. Recovering at home, I was returned to Hrastovac for convalescence. For the first time I realized what it meant to suffer and come back; for the first time I was pained by "Cannot" and "Never," especially that terrifyingly ominous "Never!" I still felt weak on my feet.

In the garden I watched gorgeous admiral butterflies suck the honeysweet Salzburg pears which covered the ground. I experienced tapping woodpeckers, singing crickets, the soft, silent travel of clouds. Everything felt new, unfamiliar. I had left the garden young and healthy; I found it now old and sick, like myself. Dry foliage rustled

along the well-kept paths. Smiljka had become a function of my delirium and fever; I thought of her now as dead. As I recovered, my old
forays became my fountain of youth. As though I were on an island:
the pole-fence around the courtyard became coastal rocks, the church
a harbor, its towers lighthouses. The poultry became happy Phaeacians, peasant carts on the dusty highway, ships on a stormy sea. Oh,
what balm can spill into a soft young soul at the sound of Zagreb bells
through a library window, as the wind brings up and takes back the
mournful, happy, and lachrymose tintinnabulations. . . .

By now the barber had taken a wife. By day or night one heard
Frau von Golubić singing: *"Das ist die Liebe, die ganz allein . . ."*
["That is the love which alone . . ."]. From that, schoolmaster Jelić
judged the *Gnädige Frau* to be a Hungarian who, during her great
travels, had done little with her hands. She called at the rectory, but
uncle said he must forgo rice after seeing her powdery, whitened face.
I could not look at her, either. Especially at those eyes which drooped
like pants without buttons. It's all as may be now; but rumor says that
the barber enjoyed a few brief golden weeks and then went mad.
Returning from Velika Gorica, where he had entered a lion's cage on
a wager, he heard strange sounds coming from the bridal chamber.
The lower half of the window was covered; so he climbed out on a
plum tree, where he was seen by the serving girl Barica. When the
Gnädige Frau led the new postal clerk forth from the chamber to
strains of her theme song, she found her husband beneath the tree,
dead of a broken neck. The villagers did not all credit Barica's version.
The lord of Čučnik told me that the sinister barber had wagered with
the postman: at midnight he would take a shot at an iron Christ Crucified at the crossing. Unfortunately, the bullet ricocheted and hit him
in the throat. The day of the funeral was marked by high wind, and
Šimek the bellringer asserted that the barber had turned into a spirit
and had been seen riding a cloud in the direction of Okić. Today, *Gnädige Frau* Golubić operates the postoffice and no longer sings *"Das ist
die Liebe. . . ."*

One night before autumn, in between the holy days of St. Pulcheria
and St. Hyacinth, an untimely bell aroused us from sleep. Many frightened people clustered around the church. Fire! There were shouts, particularly those of angry women who sounded as if their tresses were
aflame. Cattle lowed and roamed around the churchyard. My uncle
came running, looking pale and clothed only in shirt and drawers. Yet
when things calmed down, there was uncle with a stranger, laughing

till he cried. The stranger indifferently tossed his belongings beside me on the leather divan, chattering away, every now and then hugging Uncle Grga.

"You ask, what's new in Zagreb. Not much that I can see after five days in the swallow's nest. Women have begun to serve in the army, mostly in the cavalry. A horse took Ban Jelačić for a ride. A winged snake devoured St. George, becoming sufficiently fat to qualify for election to the Maksimir parliament. One inn now serves mass. Mr. Ivić on Kaptol plucks chickens and says that he will see *you* named canon, instead of him. . . ."

The fellow's tone was calm and even, as if submitting a bid.

"Enough, Zefir, enough! *Virga domini!* Ho, ho! Do all of our family have worms in the head? Ha, ha, oh, *Virga!*" Uncle embraced the man like a son.

This, then, was Zefir Zefirinović, our shirt-tail cousin: small, elegant, handsome, with curly hair, with reddish beard, upturned nose, fine white teeth, mischievous grey eyes. The larger the family, the more legendary its personalities. I was, in fact, glad to meet this chap, about whom I had heard so many good (and bad) things. By night this Zefir once cut off the locks of a provincial cousin and sold them to a barber! There was something girlish, childlike, impudent in his manner; evidently (as they say), he had taken a leaf from the Devil's book, for he seemed to be up twenty-four hours a day. He came, via Italy, from a place where he had spent a full ten years; Madrid to be precise.

Tončika came running up with a blessing and a question: "have you settled down by now?"

"No, thank God. I'm neither engaged nor married, nor do I covet the lot of any aristocrat. As you know, I belled the announcement of my own lofty arrival. Šimek and Andraš, are they still around? And is that you, Julije, golden cannoneer? I see that my vein of family life is not quite dead. Take it from me, little far-off brother, avoid angular women: go for the horizontals or, if you can find them, the verticals . . . Sad, sad, that I should not have lived during the Thirty Years' War. . . ."

After eating like a hungry thresher, he dispatched aunt and uncle to bed and began to paper his room with photos—all women seeking mates.

"As you see, golden cannoneer, I incline toward Islam." Pictures of women occupied an entire wall. "Here are Goya's *Caprichos*. What have you to say of that garroted idler's head? The great and terrible

Goya is my man. Because of him I traversed beautiful sunny Spain, where priests abound as in Croatia and where ears are even more plentiful. However, the case is not yet proven. What kind of Croat are *you:* Catholic, Muslim, Serb, Jew? I am a Croatian Croat."

He went out until dawn, then slept until evening.

I saw little of him. For whole days he roved the countryside, painting peasants and cows; often riding bareback on uncle's white-muzzled horse and going cross-country. One morning he asked: "Do you know a postal clerk named Horn?"

"Yes."

"Good. Last night I visited his place, and henceforth he is *triple* horn! A Hungarian woman wants me to paint her. But she is less than horizontal; even beneath water level!"

On the eighth day of Zefir's merry sojourn, the cows returned without Andraš. We found him about midnight by Mačji Jarak glade, lying on his stomach by a wooden well and whispering incoherently in a sort of religious trance. Occasionally he cried out, whether for pain or pleasure. Several old peasant women nearby chanted ecstatically to the Virgin. Next day enough people went there to make it look like an absolution—whole processions of psalm-singers, local clergy: every one distinctly saw the Virgin in the well.

The newspapers, too, discussed the miracle. Uncle went twice to Zagreb, to consult the hierarchy. Those nights several women gave birth; people from all over Croatia mobbed our Lady of Help. For two weeks Hrastovac surpassed Our Lady of Bistrica at the busy summer season.

The cat had washed all day. Uncle burned his right index finger while using a barometer . . . Then, in a warm evening rain, a distinguished guest arrived and was introduced as Dr. Hagen, a Christian archeologist from Germany. He requested uncle to show him, that very evening if possible, any old church pieces, which he offered to replace with new ones (and to pay additionally, if necessary). Dr. Hagen collected church antiquities throughout the entire *kaj*-speaking area.

Uncle promised two shabby old chalices and invited Hagen to stay. Such Croatian hospitality pleased the archeologist. At supper, before joining in our pious and customary *Our Father*, he reviled Jewry with ugly stories and jokes—the Jew and the capon, the Jew and the pepper, Smuggler Jake and the robbers—the fare was more peppery than in some rich Benedictine monastery. Aunt Tončika left the table, in accordance with English custom. We smiled at the skillful use of Yiddish dialect. It was as if Abraham had wished to slay *him*, rather than a sheep. The man's elegance owed something to fragrant soap and to cosmetic aids; but his culture was magisterially German. The anti-Semite spoke as many languages as did the Twelve Apostles. It all overwhelmed uncle to such an extent that he allowed his own bed, *prie-Dieu*, and other personal items to be transferred into the "palace."

The next day, while I was resting, my Spanish brother arrived with—a gun. "Come with me and quickly. *Testis unus testis nullus* ["One witness is not enough"]."

In the garden we climbed secretly until we could get a good look through the ivy into the "palace." The sight astounded us: our archeologist had draped himself over Uncle Grga's armchair and was drinking wine from the venerable chalice. His bare legs, which resembled not so much X-rays as some O-ray yet undiscovered, rested on the crucifix of the *prie-Dieu*. A stole and dalmatic covered his lumpy back. Chuckling, he read from Grga's missal as if from the *Budapest Caviar*, with a black preaching tricorne tipped over one ear. I could not believe my eyes; it must be a dream, an illusion.

"Can you see Big Nose?"

Boom! went Zefir's carbine. The mighty archeologist turned as sallow as a blackbird's beak. There was banging on the door. Uncle's voice could be heard, from his room: "*Was is' das?* Open the door, great learned one!"

"Break it down if he tries to kill himself!" yelled Zefir. The door yielded, and through it went Uncle Grga with his new Bosnian smoking apparatus. We entered by the window. The archeologist was almost without a stitch and trembling like Adam being expelled from Paradise. Scholars may not be quarrelsome; but Hagen had long, pendent ears, and it is well-known that long-eared animals are cowards. His legs resembled trumpets, his stomach a tympanum. His eyes looked down along an ocarinalike nose, and he had lowered his fat hands modestly to serve as a fig leaf. Now, all this strange orchestra was in pause, like an aspic. From the cabinet the stuffed two-headed calf gaped down and seemed to ask with its glass eyes: what were two golden bishop's caps doing on *its* calflike head?

Silence. Then, rolling his eyes, Uncle Grga roared: "Sacrilege and abomination! Magyarism! *Schweinerei!*"

"By my mother and father!" mumbled the abashed and panic-

stricken interloper. By raising his locked hands, he mutely acknowledged that more than his father had been Jewish. He was ensnared like
a pig in a poke.

"God ... Holy Virgin ... how dreadful!" The whispered words
issued from behind me and came from my aunt, who stood in a white-
white nightcap and viewed the naked man as Judith must have viewed
Holofernes in the tent. She fainted upon the tricolored rag rug.

"An Iscariot ... He must be thrashed!" Uncle's eyes ground like
millstones. He breathed heavily. The new Bosnian pipe sailed forth
and struck the archeologist. At that moment Tončika returned to con-
sciousness. What a black pastry had rolled into the pig's sack!

"Yai!"

With a howl, the scholar leaped higher than the astonished twin-
headed calf. So lightly did Uncle Grga tap him! "You shall pay, you
antiquarian wretch!" Uncle was hoarse by now. He moved for the
catch of his gun. The glorious archeologist must have been a skilled
acrobat, for he flew through the window like a shot. Hastily dressing
in the stable, he climbed into Andraš's cart and must surely have
arrived in good time at Samobor; for Zefir had stuck a lighted cigarette
under the donkey's tail. The cart took off straining at every iron bolt.

We later heard that a Dr. Hagen had vilified middle-class Croats in
the pages of the *Pester Lloyd*. A bedbug never stinks so badly as when
you squash it.

The village smelled of hemp, the foliage was thinning and the
grape-crop turning to red or black when Zefir finished decorating the
chapel of the Virgin by the Well. The local gentry were on eggshells:
everyone wanted to view the work. But to enhance the surprise, Zefir
covered everything with doormats and kept the key with him. When
the longed-for day finally arrived, Crkvica and Mačji Jarak were as full
of people as a fig is full of seeds. Expectation had turned everyone pale.

"Donkey ... *virga* ... *Dominus vobiscum*," uncle whispered at the
end of mass. I was serving and repressed a smile. There on the wall
was Noah, the first drunk, and (except for a beard) the spitting image
of Grga. *Gnädige Frau* von Golubić was Potiphar, who dragged
Andraš of Čučnik by the collar. The donkey was our own; teacher Jelić
sat him enroute to Jerusalem, and the background Jews were local
peasants. Šimek the bellringer carried Herod's crown, and a short reddish Count looked paler as he munched grasshoppers in the desert. The
wretch had painted me as an innocent child. Aunt Tončika (her hair
cut short) was Pontius Pilate; Dr. Mauruš, a devil or tempter. The Hon-

orable Dark One wooed the pure Suzanna (our cook!). The Twelve
Apostles were the twelve nearest parish priests, while the three Magi
were farm workers at a Hrastovac estate.

The sinful allusions stung uncle and a few others. But the workmanship was so good that everyone looked for the artist. In vain. Zefir had
left without a trace! Back home, we found Andraš and the cook weeping in the kitchen.

According to them, Zefir had committed suicide. The gun had gone
off just fifteen minutes earlier. Copious tears. Following uncle into the
book-browsery, my breath left my body: Zefir lay on the floor, clad in
a shirt, a kerchief over his eyes, a fallen gun beside him. His face was
bone-white, his chest grey; over the heart a wound oozed blood. I fell
upon my dear relative, while uncle turned away. . . .

At that point, he casually jumped to his feet and, with a smile, began
to wipe off his makeup. "I'm not mad enough to die, when I'm so well
esteemed by the golden cannoneer and Uncle Grga."

"*Virga Domini*, this wild man and rascal has done it again. Enough,
enough of these dirty tricks!"

In Hrastovac we looked forward to a drink of must and cooked
chestnut with honey.

. . .

Autumn clouds, white and heavy like wool . . . The landscape began
to look yellow, like that in old Gobelin tapestries. Autumn clouded both
windows and eyes with moisture. Soon winter frost would settle on the
bare ruined branches, bringing with it new cares. When he said good-
bye, uncle did not cross the threshold; instead, lacking strength, he
stood back and whispered, "may reputation and honor ever outweigh
a shameful moment or hour or lifetime." Tončika sobbed. Swiping desperately with his pipe, uncle sent us away and turned his back. Yet I
saw a blue kerchief emerge from his pocket.

Zefir whistled, Šimek cracked his whip, the horses stretched their
bellies and leaped forward. Behind us Hrastovac faded into memory.

VII

Returning five years later from Vienna, where father had sent me,
I found Uncle Grga in his garden.

He seemed taciturn. Age and blindness had taken their toll; he scarcely recognized me. But there were a number of questions, because we had not corresponded as distant relatives should.

"What has become of Zefir?"

"Gone. Left the country." No one knew more. The chaplain had died long ago in Gleichenberg.

"And Aunt Tončika?"

The pipe moved feebly in the direction of the church. I understood. At the cemetery, I did not find her at first, for she was buried near the noble Štijef Zugec, in a crypt. On a nearby grave, with a simple peasant cross that bore a paper likeness of the Virgin of Bistrica (along with a box of holy water and a cup of oil without a wick), I read the name "Jelić Smiljana . . ."

The wind blew, stirring the ivy on the mound. It was as if Smiljka had awakened and was telling Tončika or Zugec about black mares or white horses. On the church towers, doves cooed. A single, soft marble cloud moved toward the mountains of Samobor.

Again the ivy trembled, suggesting speech. A bug arose from a flower, whirred and buzzed and showed gold in the light, then moved skyward . . . and disappeared.

Losing it from view, I bent to pick several ivy leaves. These faded fragments are all that remain of my youth. Yet there are people who do not possess as much. . . .

Notes and References

Chapter One

1. Walter Lippmann, *The Public Philosophy* (New York: Mentor Books, 1956), pp. 12, 16.
2. Charles and Barbara Jelavich, *The Balkans* (Englewood, N.J.: Prentice-Hall, 1965), p. 60.
3. Ibid., p. 70.
4. Mirko Žeželj, *Tragajući za Matošem* [Searching for Matoš] (Zagreb, 1970). The doggerel began: "Hédervary/Niš ne mari . . ." (Hédervary doesn't care . . .").
5. In one story, the Matoš-character says: "Of all the sections of his native city . . . Grič was his favorite." See A. G. Matoš, *Sabrana djela* [Collected Works], ed. Dragutin Tadijanović et al., 20 vols. (Zagreb, 1976), 2:58. Henceforth this edition will be cited throughout by volume and page.
6. 2:146–48.
7. 2:147.
8. See the introduction to *Hrvatska književna kritika*, vol. 4, *Kritike Antuna Gustava Matoša* [Croatian Literary Criticism, vol. 4, Criticisms by A. G. Matoš], ed. Marijan Matković, 2d ed. (Zagreb, 1962), esp. pp. 10–11.
9. 5:121. See also chapter 4 below.
10. 20:123–63.
11. For a sample of the correspondence, see 19:54–55.
12. In his essay, "Bishop Strossmayer's Memorial," part of the collection *Vidici i putovi* [Look-outs and High Roads, 1907] in 4:25.
13. Materials on Matoš's life include his autobiography (as far as 1897) in 5:289–93; the article "Matoš" by "T. L." in *Enciklopedija Jugoslavije* (Zagreb, 1965); the essay by Velibor Gligorić in *U vihoru* [In the Whirlwind] (Belgrade, 1962), pp. 7–128, and his article in *Antun Gustav Matoš*, ed. Tode Čolak (Belgrade, 1965), pp. 17–43. See also Žeželj, *Tragajući za Matošem*.
One brother, Felix, died young. The others were Leon (1878–1947), Milan (1887–1960), and a sister Danica (1876–1961).
14. A stylized version of the escape is given in the story "After a New God," in 2:304–5. Other accounts occur in Matoš's "Reminiscences," 4:261, and in "My Prisons," 5:157.
15. 4:15. Two stories, "The Odyssey" and "A Terrible Wager," were published in *Pobratim*. The first concerns a young man who returns home from Texas; the second, the misadventures of a barber who has undertaken to cut off the nose of a corpse.

16. 4:15–16.

17. 3:68–69. "Black Cat" was a restaurant in Paris. The Dardanelles stood until 1902.

18. 19:268–71.

19. 8:50–57, 61–65.

20. 4:16.

21. Gligorić, *U vihoru,* p. 9.

22. 3:83.

23. 3:345–76. The essay was first published in *Nada* (1901), then reprinted in Matoš's *Ogledi* [Perspectives, 1905].

24. For further details, see Barbara Tuchman, *The Proud Tower* (New York: MacMillan, 1966), pp. 171–226.

25. *Iverje, Novo iverje,* and *Umorne priče* comprise vol. 1 of the *Collected Works.*

26. 2:39, 58.

27. 3:301.

28. 4:47–72. The primary version is sometimes quite different. Left out of *Ogledi* [Perspectives], it was not reprinted until 1955.

29. See his notes and annotated references, in vols. 17 and 18.

30. 17:263–65.

31. See vols. 19 and 20, also edited by Davor Kapetanić.

32. 19:147, 183; 20:173.

33. 19:352.

34. 15:82. The most influential Belgrade journal was Skerlić's *Srpski književni glasnik. Dnevni list* and *Odjek* were independent. The radicals controlled *Samouprava.*

35. 4:14, 22, 126.

36. 19:221.

37. 5:271.

38. 15:94, 97, 104.

39. 9:41–44, 45–52.

40. 4:22–26, 47–72.

41. In the essay "Barrès and the Barrès-Drunkard," 12:275. "The Disciple" charges Ujević with ingratitude, 12:267.

42. 12:311.

43. All are in vol. 2.

44. 4:286. Elsewhere, Matoš argues that life is only *material* for art; see 12:242.

45. 4:221.

46. See his essay "The Twilight of Romanticism," 9:192–98.

47. 9:167 (Rousseau); 4:248 and 6:145 (Kranjčević).

48. Cf. 11:83: "Artistically speaking, Meštrović is a Serb or, to be precise, a 'Yugoslav.' . . ."

49. 4:118.

50. The travel pieces are collected in vol. 11.

51. See footnote 41 above and chap. 3 below, esp. nn. 89 and 90.

52. 11:306.

53. 17:9, 121.

54. 3:262.

55. Among notable articles on Zagreb are "At Home" (1905), 4:27; "Zagreb Singular and Plural" (1912), 5:175; "Zagreb by Day" (1909), 11:175. See also "A Zagreb Guidebook" (1911), 2:146.

56. 8:309.

57. 20:67, in a letter (22 September 1907) to Milan Ogrizović.

58. 16:60. In an earlier essay "Our Literary Crisis" (1909), he complains not that modernism is Croatian, but that it is cliquish. See 6:200.

59. In *Vihor*, 1 May 1914, p. 89.

Chapter Two

1. A. G. Matoš, *Sabrana djela* [Collected Works], vol. 1.

2. See the editor's notes, 2:293 and 295.

3. Such as "First Song," 2:39–51, and "A Light Went Out," 1:161–65, both with a soirée setting.

4. Professor William Huie of Corpus Christi University was kind enough to discuss these points in a personal letter to me. See also Theodore Perry, *Filmguide to 8½* (Bloomington: Indiana University Press, 1975).

5. See Ludwig Wittgenstein, *Philosophical Grammar*, ed. Rush Rhees, trans. Anthony Kenny (Berkeley: University of California Press, 1974); also, his *Lectures and Conversations on Aesthetics, Psychology, and Religious Belief*, ed. Cyril Barrett (Berkeley: University of California Press, 1967). Dreams were a translation game played by dreamers. Wittgenstein believed that an effective dream grammar would permit translation *into* and *out of* the dream mode.

6. 1:198–99.

7. It seems that Milica (or "Lila," in the story of that title) generally keeps her comments to herself and does not fight the system. But she does tell the narrator that her former lover was impotent (*vudren*, "like a wet rag"). 2:139.

8. 2:73.

9. 2:29–35.

10. There are conversations with the dead in "Autumn Idyll" and "Paradiso." See 1:204–25, 2:172–76.

11. 2:54–57.

12. 1:67.

13. 1:254.

14. 1:104.

15. Ibid.

16. 11:181.

17. 1:230.

18. 1:184; also p. 300, n. 49.

19. 1:185.

20. See 1:291. Smiljka's schoolmaster father, with a passion for birding and gardening, is Gustav's parent August. The writer Fran Mažuranić (1859–1928) is protrayed in "Path to Nowhere," and perhaps elsewhere in *Umorne priče*. See 1:166–69, 247–58. Count Andrija in "A Light Went Out" is said to be modeled on Matoš's bohemian friend from Paris, Meczyslaw Goldberg, 1:161–65.

21. 1:77–78.

22. 2:22–28, 114–21.

23. 2:12–21.

24. 1:190–93 and 2:108–13.

25. Matoš gives the most extended version of his esthetics in correspondence with the author and playwright Milan Ogrizović in 1907. See 20:42–45, 53–55, 66–68. A compendious restatement of Matoš's values is given by Tadijanović in 1:279–81. Since symbols were greater than reality, Matoš could argue that, for a symbolist, reality was only half-truth.

26. Letter (14 September 1909) to Vladimir Lunaček, 19:245. On other occasions Matoš professed to be self-taught.

27. 20:54.

28. 20:68.

29. 1:80.

30. 1:81.

31. 2:218.

32. Ivo Frangeš, "Stil Matoševe novelistike" ["Matoš's Storytelling Art"] in *Rad/JAZU* [Works of the Yugoslav Academy of Science and Art] 333 (1963): separate issue.

Chapter Three

1. A. G. Matoš, *Sabrana djela* [Collected Works], vols. 3–4. See also the following: vols. 6–7: *O hrvatskoj književnosti* [Croatian Literature]; vol. 8: *O srpskoj književnosti* [Serbian Literature], vol. 9: *O stranim književnostima* [Foreign Literatures], vol. 11: *Putopisi* [Travel Pieces], vols. 15–16: *Feljtoni, impresije, članci* [Feuilletons, Impressions, Articles].

Dragi naši savremenici [Our Dear Contemporaries], vol. 12, is a collection by Matoš, but includes material by others.

Pečalba [Day Labor], vol. 5, Matoš's last book, contains some articles pertinent to this chapter.

2. Letter (30 March 1911) to Marko Car, 19:62. For contrary opinions see 3:136 and 4:283.

3. Augustin Ujević, *Sabrana djela* [Collected Works], (Zagreb, 1967), 16:83.

4. Ibid., p. 65.

5. Letter (3 December 1902) to Vladimir Tkalčić, 20:157.

6. Letter (23 February 1902) to Vladimir Tkalčić, 20:146.

7. Letter (15 December 1909) to Hilda Fürstenburg, 19:108.

8. 3:71.

9. 3:186.

10. From the introduction to *The Portable Poe* by Phillip Van Doren Stern (New York, Viking Portable Library, 1973), p. xxxvi.

11. 3:236, 314, 371; 9:178. Rousseau had a feminine sensibility, but was too self-centered to understand love.

12. 3:199.

13. 4:101.

14. 4:102.

15. 4:94.

16. 11:252.

17. 3:103–222, 283–90.

18. 3:288–89.

19. 3:120.

20. 3:117.

21. 3:284.

22. 3:283.

23. Letter (no date, October 1894) to Leon Matoš, 19:282–83.

24. Mihovil Kombol, *Poviest hrvatske književnosti do narodnog preporoda* [*Croatian Literature before the National Renaissance*] (Zagreb: Matica hrvatska, 1945), p. 7.

25. 4:27.

26. 4:46.

27. Ujević, p. 72.

28. 4:41 and 5:58.

29. 11:275–76.

30. 4:110, 111.

31. For material on Barrès, see Geoffrey Brereton, *Short History of French Literature* (Baltimore: Penguin Books, 1968); L. Cazamian, *A History of French Literature* (London: Oxford University Press, 1955); Helmut Hatzfeld, *Trends and Styles in Twentieth Century French Literature* (rev. ed., Washington: Catholic University of America, 1966); Albert Thibaudet, *French Literature from 1795 to Our Era*, trans. by Charles Lam Markmann (New York: Funk and Wagnalls, 1938).

32. Quoted by Matoš in 9:214.

33. 9:215.

34. 9:214.

35. A. G. Matoš, *Hrvatska književna kritika*, vol. 4, *Kritike Antuna Gus-*

tava Matoša [*Croatian Literary Criticism*, vol. 4, *Criticisms by A. G. Matoš*], p. 18.

36. Quoted by Antun Barac in *Antun Gustav Matoš*, ed. Tode Čolak (Belgrade, 1965), p. 88.

37. Letter (3 May 1904) to Andrija Milčinović, 20:388.

38. 4:286.

39. 4:59.

40. 4:61.

41. 4:290.

42. 4:270–71.

43. 4:274.

44. Letter (11 September 1906) from Milan Ogrizović, 20:22.

45. 4:175.

46. 4:178.

47. 8:153.

48. 4:221–22.

49. 19:350, 375; 20:152. Furthermore, Kranjčević was an editor of *Nada* in Sarajevo and in that capacity had rejected articles by Matoš on occasion.

50. 4:414, n. 229.

51. 4:155.

52. 4:237.

53. 5:178.

54. 5:176.

Chapter Four

1. The best edition is that edited by Dragutin Tadijanović: A. G. Matoš, *Sabrana djela* [Collected Works], vol. 5, *Pjesme, Pečalba* (Zagreb, 1976). All references are to this source, by volume and page. But citations are given only where parts of a poem are quoted. For original titles, see the bibliography.

Tadijanović 5:297–312, discusses these predecessors of the *Collected Works:* (1) *Pjesme* [Poems] (Zagreb, 1923); (2) *Djela* [Works], vol. 5, *Pjesme i epigrami* [Poems and Epigrams], ed. Antun Barac (Zagreb, 1938); (3) *Izabrane pjesme* [Selected Poems], ed. Gustav Krklec (Zagreb, 1950); (4) *Sabrana djela* [Collected Works], ed. Dragutin Tadijanović (Zagreb, 1953); (5) *Izabrane pjesme* [Selected Poems], ed. Dragutin Tadijanović, introduction by Jure Kaštelan (1954); 2d ed., Zagreb, 1962; this was the edition published under the auspices of *Matica hrvatska;* (6) *Pjesme, Pripovijesti, Autobiografija* [Poems, Stories, Autobiography], ed. Dragutin Tadijanović, and Marijan Matković (Zagreb, 1967).

The epigrams are collected in vol. 12: *Dragi naši Savremenici* [Our Dear Contemporaries].

2. Antun Barac, "Matoševa lirika" [Matoš's Poetry], in *Savremenik* (1919), p. 467.

3. 5:121.

4. In this line, the predicate *(po hiži me hinca)* precedes the subject *(mislih črni roj)*. More particularly, the inversion *mislih črni roj* (lit., "of thoughts-black-hive") is awkward.

5. See 5:321–22.

6. 5:50–51.

7. 5:49.

8. Years later, Edmund Wilson in *Axel's Castle* (New York: Charles Scribner's Sons, 1931), pp. 1–25, defined symbolism in terms of the reclusive hero of Villier de l'Isle Adam's poetic drama. According to C. M. Bowra, symbolist poets "attempted to convey a supernatural experience in the language of visible things." Words were therefore used to evoke a reality beyond the senses. C. M. Bowra, *The Heritage of Symbolism* (London: St. Martin, 1943), p. 5.

9. 12:252.

10. 5:58.

11. Ivo Andrić, "A. G. Matoš," *Vihor*, 1 May 1914, p. 91.

12. Slavko Mihalić and Ivan Kušan, *La poésie croate des origines à nos jours* (Paris: P. Seghers, 1972), p. 116.

13. Olga Grahor, *France in the Work and Ideas of Antun Gustav Matoš* (Munich: Otto Sagner, 1973).

14. See 5:10, 65.

15. Elaine Marks, ed., *French Poetry from Baudelaire to the Present* (New York: Laurel Language Library, 1962), p. 15.

16. 4:55.

17. See Robert Nisbet, *Sociology as an Art Form* (London: Oxford University Press, 1976), esp. p. 63.

18. Augustin Ujević, "U spomen A. G. Matošu" ["In Memory of A. G. Matoš"], in *Savremenik* (1914), p. 112.

19. 5:92.

20. 5:81.

21. 5:63. See also pp. 130–31, where he mounts an attack on "Ogrizina" (Milan Ogrizović) in ten-syllable verse.

22. 1:265. See Jure Kaštelan, "Lirika A. G. Matoša" [Matoš's Poetry] *Rad/JAZU* [*Works of the Yugoslav Academy of Science and Art*] 310 (1957): 60.

23. This has been explored in detail by Ivo Frangeš. See his "Stil Matoševe novelistike" [Matoš's Storytelling Art], *Rad/JAZU* [Works of the Yugoslav Academy of Science and Art] 333 (1963).

Chapter Five

1. See in particular: Augustin Ujević, "Hrvatska knjiga" ["Croatian Literature"], in *Stekliš* (Zagreb, 1911); "Em smo Horvati" [We Are Croats Still],

Savremenik, May 1914; and the various articles in *Sabrana djela* [Collected Works] (Zagreb, 1967), vol. 16. Henceforth this edition will be cited only by volume and page. Ivo Andrić, "A. G. Matoš," *Vihor,* 1 May 1914, pp. 89–91; Velibor Gligorić, "A. G. Matoš," in his *U vihoru* [In the Whirlwind] Belgrade, 1962, pp. 7–128; Olga Grahor, *France in the Works and Ideas of A. G. Matoš* (Munich: Otto Sagner, 1973); Marijan Matković, *Hrvatska književna kritika* [*Croatian Literary Criticism*], vol. 4, *Kritike Antuna Gustava Matoša* [*Criticism by A. G. Matoš*], 2d ed. (Zagreb, 1962), especially the introductory essay, "A. G. Matoš kao kritičar" [A. G. Matoš as a Critic], pp. 5–24; Tode Čolak, ed., *Antun Gustav Matoš* (Belgrade, 1965), a collection of essays by various hands; Mirko Žeželj, *Tragajući za Matošem* [Searching for Matoš] (Zagreb, 1970).

More specific evaluations are provided by Jure Kaštelan, "Lirika A. G. Matoša" [The Poetry of A. G. Matoš], in *Rad/JAZU* [*Works of the Yugoslav Academy of Science and Art*], 310 (1957); and Ivo Frangeš, "Stil Matoševe novelistike" [Matoš's Storytelling Art], ibid., vol. 333 (1963).

2. Quoted in Gligorić, *U vihoru,* p. 103.

3. Andrić, in *Vihor,* 1 May 1914, p. 91.

4. For a synopsis, see Žeželj, *Tragajući za Matošem,* pp. 466–67.

5. Ibid., p. 467.

6. But he told Milan Ogrizović in a letter (28 July 1907) that " . . . only what is in book-form should be considered literary . . . Matoš the journalist is of no great account." See 20:43.

7. In Hindu religion, there are three aspects of Brahma: creation, conservation, destruction (corresponding to Brahma, Vishnu, and Shiva). In "At Home," a teenage Zagreb tough "with clean shirt and dirty soul" shakes his fist at the visitor Matoš, who calls him "a trimurti of dog, monkey, and reptile"—a resident Croat who embodies the worst national traits.

8. Gligorić, *U vihoru,* p. 128.

9. See the introduction to A. G. Matoš, *Izabrana djela* [Selected Works], edited by Tode Čolak (Belgrade 1963), pp. 10, 13, 16.

10. Matoš's opinion is expressed in a letter (14 September 1909) to Vladimir Lunaček, 19:245.

11. Most of these examples come from the essay "Lobor," 4:93.

12. Davor Kapetanić, editor of the notebooks and letters, has preserved the misspellings in vols. 17–20. In fact, all the *Sabrana djela* have special vocabulary sections.

13. Gligorić, *U vihoru,* p. 17.

14. Letter (28 July 1907) to Milan Ogrizović, 20:44.

15. Letter (22 August 1907) to Milan Ogrizović, 20:54.

16. Andrić, *Vihor,* 1 May 1914, p. 90.

17. Žeželj, *Tragajući za Matošem,* p. 465.

18. Gligorić, *U vihoru,* p. 37; see also p. 121.

19. The fat clergyman Frntić in "Fresh Cracknels!" lives in a room smelling of rosemary and mildewed leather; his housekeeper has three boys who look like him; he is hypochondriacal, in fear of a stroke, 1:38.

The portrait of Grga Alagović in "A Time to Remember" is more sympathetically drawn, possibly because it incorporated features both of Matoš's grandfather and of Ante Pinterović. But the priest "reeked of smoke and tobacco"; he liked to drink and live well, 1:76–77. For a translation, see the appendix.

20. In the essay "Young Croatia" (1912), 16:51. See also the comments in Gligorić, *U vihoru*, p. 123.

21. 18:219. For further descriptions of Dis, see 4:189 and 8:277 and 290. From the Belgrade days, Matoš remembered Dis for his intense eyes, curly hair, and thin face.

22. Quoted by Gligorić, *U vihoru*, p. 64.

23. For references to "Šeširljić," see 1:184 and 10:29. For the other references, see 10:36 and 3:184. Cf. also: "The rug of Mr. N. will soon give birth (he masturbates)," 17:10; and "Jews mention God's name only in the city, not in the village," 18:24.

He is on more solid ground when in a more genial mood. He imagined the Eiffel Tower as some giant's toothpick. He teased Zagreb innkeepers with reversing the miracle of Caana. Christ had turned water to wine, but they regularly turned wine into water!

24. Matković, *Hrvatska književna kritika*, 4:6.

25. 17:264.

Selected Bibliography

PRIMARY SOURCES

Sabrana djela [*Collected Works*]. 20 vols. Edited by Dragutin Tadijanović et al. Zagreb: Jugoslavenska Akademija Znanosti i Umjetnosti, 1976. The most recent, complete, and scholarly edition of Matoš's work; with annotations, glosses on vocabulary, and copious indices. The following volumes are of particular interest:

1. Story Collections:
Iverje (Chips, 1899): "Moć savjesti" [The Power of Conscience, 1892], "Nezahvalnost?" [Ingratitude? 1897], "Čestitka" [The Welcoming Speech, 1896], "Pereci, friški pereci" [Fresh Cracknels! 1897], "Kip domovine let 188–" [Statue of the Motherland, Summer 1888–, 1895], "Miš" (Mouse, 1899)
Novo iverje [Fresh Chips, 1900]: "Nekad bilo—sad se spominjalo" [A Time to Remember, 1900], "U čudnim gostima" [Among Strangers, 1898], "Camao" [The Parrot, 1900], "Božićna priča" [A Christmas Story, 1900], "Iglasto čeljade" [A Needlelike Man, 1900], "Samotna noć" [Lonely Night, 1900]
Umorne priče [Tales from Weariness, 1909]: "Moć štampe" [Power of the Press, 1904], "Ugasnulo svjetlo" [A Light Went Out, 1902], "Bura u tišini" [Storm in Quietness, 1901], "Duševni covjek" [A Man of Conscience, 1902], "Lijepa Jelena" [Pretty Helen, 1906], "On" [The Great Man, 1903], "Poštenje" [A Matter of Honor, 1901], "Balkon" [The Balcony, 1902], "Jesenska idila" [Autumn Idyll, 1903], "Prijatelj" [The Friend, 1907], "Ministarsko tijesto" [A Minsterial Pâté, 1906], "Vrabac" [The Sparrow, 1902], "Osveta ogledala" [The Mirror's Revenge, 1907], "Ubio!" [I Have Killed Her! 1904], "Put u ništa" [Path to Nowhere, 1902], "Cvijet sa raskršća" [Flower from the Crossing, 1902], "Sjena" [Shadows, 1908]

2. Uncollected Stories
Novele, Humoreske, Satire [Stories, Humoresques, Satires]: "D-Dur Sonata" [Sonata in D-Major, 1892], "Odisije" [The Odyssey, 1895], "Strašna oklada" [A Terrible Wager, 1895], "Nasamarili ga" [A Deceiver Deceived, 1895], "Prva pjesma" [First Song, 1901], "Bijeda" [Poverty, 1902], "Za novim bogom" [After a New God, 1902], "Prva nevjera"

[First Infidelity, 1903], "Uskrsnuće bez Uskrsa" [Resurrection without Easter, 1909], "Život za milijune" [A Life Worth Millions, 1909], "Presvijetli ražnjić" [A Skewer for His Excellency!, 1909], "Sve se događa" [Everything Happens, 1911], "Lila" [Lila, 1911], "Moralista" [The Moralist, 1911], "Zagrebački Baedeker" [A Zagreb Guidebook, 1911], "Ljubav i dubljina" [Love and the Deeps, 1911], "Običan događaj" [A Common Story, 1912], "Susjeda" [The Neighbor, 1913], "Klobuk" [The Stovepipe Hat, 1913], "Za narod" [For the People, 1924]

3. Essay Collections (titles without dates are posthumous; selective titles)
Vol. 3: *Ogledi* [Perspectives, 1905], "Imaginarno putovanje" [An Imaginary Journey], "Stendhal" [Henry Beyle], "Književnost i batine" [Beatings in Literature], "Vergl" [Barrel Organs]
Vol. 4: *Vidici i putovi* [Look-outs and High Roads, 1907], "Don Kihot' [Don Quixote], "Janko Veselinović," "Suton kazališta" [Twilight of the Theater], "Strossmayerov spomenik" [Bishop Strossmayer's Memorial], "Kod kuće" [At Home], "Baudelaire," "Siesta." *Naši ljudi i krajevi* [Our People at Home, 1910], "Oko Lobora" [Lobor], "Iz Samobora" [Samobor], "Oko Rijeke" [Rijeka], Stevan Sremac, "O izgubljenom nosu" [A Lost Nose], "Žarko Jovan Ilić," "Srpski modernista" [Milan Ćurčin, Serbian Modernist], "Jovan Skerlić," "Lirika Sime Pandurovića" [The Poetry of Sima Pandurovic], "U žutoj kući" [In the Little Yellow House], "Hyperions Tod" [Hyperion's Death], "Sintetične kritike" [Milan Marjanović's *Synthetic Criticism*], "Župnik Pinterović" [The Parish Priest, Ante Pinterović], "U sjeni velikog imena" [In the Shadow of A Great Name], "Uspomene" [Reminiscences], "Narodna kultura" [National Culture], "Književnost i književnici" [Books and Authors], "Slikar Crnčić" [The Painter K. M. Crnčić]
Vol. 5: *Pečalba* [Day Labor, 1913], "Zagreb i Zagrebi" [Zagreb, Singular and Plural], "Proljetna ćaskanja" [Spring Chatter], "Društvenost" [Social Life], "Ladanjske večeri" [Country Evenings], "Pariška kronika" [Paris Chronicle], "Moji zatvori" [My Prisons], "Tolstoj," "Barnum"
Vols. 6–7: *O hrvatskoj književnosti* [Croatian Literature], "Za Kranjčevića" [For Kranjčević], "August Harambašić" (in two versions), "Naša književna kriza" [Our Literary Crisis], "*Pjesme* V. Vidrića" [Poems by V. Vidrić], "Mlada Hrvatska" [Young Croatia], "Stari i mladi" [The Old and the Young]
Vol. 8. *O srpskoj književnosti* [Serbian Literature], *Hajduk Stanko* (Veselinović's *Stanko the Highwayman:* two versions), "Jovan Dučić: *Pjesme*" [Poems by J. Dučić], "Lirska šetnja" [A Poetic Walk with Milan Rakić]
Vol. 9: *O stranim književnostima* [Foreign Literatures], "Maurice Barrès," "Dvjestogodišnjica Jeana Jacquesa Rousseaua" [The Rousseau Bicentennial], "Romantični bogomrak" [The Twilight of Romanticism], "Futurizam" [Futurism]

Vol. 11: *O likovnim umjestnostima* [The Plastic Arts], "Meštrović," *Putopisi* [Travel Pieces], "Ferije" [Holidays], "Zagreb po danu" [Zagreb by Day], "Oko Križevca" [Križevac], "Obična šetnja" [An Ordinary Walk], "Campus nobilium" [A Field of Nobility], "Wahrheit und Dichtung" [Truth and Poetry], "Oko Save" [Along the Sava], "Vodom i kopnom" [By Land and By Sea], "Rimski izleti" [Roman Outings]

Vol. 12: *Dragi naši savremenici* [Our Dear Contemporaries, 1912], "Literarni fakini" [Literary Rascals], "Realizam i artizam" [Realism and Art], Discipulus [The Disciple]

Vols. 15–16: *Feljtoni, impresije, članci* [Feuilletons, Impressions, Articles], "Umjetnost i nacionalizam" [Art and Nationalism], "Književna kriza" [The Literary Crisis], "Boemski život" [The Bohemian Life], "Kult energije" [The Cult of Energy], "Mlada Hrvatska" [Young Croatia]

4. Poetry

Vol. 5: *Pjesme* [Poems], "Srodnost" [Correspondences], "Jesenje veče" [Autumn Evening], "U travi" [In the Grass], "Arhiloh" [Archilochus], "Maćuhica" [The Pansy], "Tajanstvena ruža" [A Secret Rose], "Djevojčici mjesto igračke" [To a Little Girl in Lieu of a Toy], "Prosjak" [The Beggar], "Pravda" [A True Story], "Mističan sonet" [Mystical sonnet], "Metamorfoza" [Metamorphosis], "Mladoj Hrvatskoj" [To Young Croatia], "Stara pjesma" [An Old Song], "Mora" [The Nightmare], "Utjeha kose" [Consolation from Her Tress], "Hrastovački nokturno" [A Nocturne from Hrastovac], "Kod kuće" [At Home], "Grički dijalog" [A Dialogue in Grič], "Lakrdijaš" [The Buffoon], "Gnijezdo bez sokola" [Nest Without a Falcon], "Elegija" [Elegy], "Acta Apostolorum" [Acts of the Apostles], "Lijepa smrt" [A Beautiful Death], "Notturno" [Nocturne], "Gospa Marija" [Lady Mary], "Jutarnja kiša" [Morning Rain]

5. Letters, Notebooks, Literary Letters

Dojmovi [Impressions from Abroad], vol. 3.

Bilježnice [Notebooks], vols. 17–18.

Pisma [Letters], vols. 19–20.

Izabrana djela [Selected Works]. Edited and introduced by Tode Čolak. Belgrade: Narodna knjiga, 1963. A one-volume selection of poems, stories, travel pieces, criticisms, and letters. Includes reminiscences by others and samples of the literature about Matoš, as well as a chronology and brief bibliography.

Hrvatska književna kritika. Vol. 4. *Kritike Antuna Gustava Matoša* [Croatian Literary Criticism. Vol. 4. Criticisms by A. G. Matoš]. Introduction by Marijan Matković. 2d ed. Zagreb: Matica hrvatska, 1962. Criticisms about foreign and domestic authors, essays on literary history and theory. The introduction deals with Matoš's status as a critic.

SECONDARY SOURCES

1. General Studies

ČOLAK, TODE, ed. *Antun Gustav Matoš*. Belgrade: Nolit, 1962. Articles by various hands, including Antun Barac, Velibor Gligorić, and Ivo Frangeš.

GLIGORIĆ, VELIBOR. "A. G. Matoš." In *U vihoru* [In the Whirlwind]. Belgrade: Nolit, 1962. A Serbian critic examines Tin Ujević and Miroslav Krleža, along with Matoš, in a broad survey. The study was published first in *Savremenik* 1–5 (1960).

GRAHOR, OLGA. *France in the Work and Ideas of Antun Gustav Matoš*. Munich: Otto Sagner, 1973. Although primarily a study of French influences upon Matoš, this work does cover all phases of his literary output.

T. L. "Matoš, Antun Gustav." In *Enciklopedija Jugoslavije*. Zagreb: Leksikografski-Zavod FNRJ: 1965. A brief but useful summary, with bibliography; the author emphasizes criticism.

ŽEŽELJ, MIRKO. *Tragajući za Matošem* [Searching for Matoš]. Zagreb: Matica hrvatska, 1970. A charming reconstruction of inner life, based upon authentic materials. It is hard to say where Žeželj ends and Matoš begins. No index.

2. Miscellaneous Articles and Studies

A. G. Matoš—In Memoriam o 20-godišnjici pjesnikove smrti [In Memoriam: Twenty Years]. Zagreb, 1934. Articles by Antun Barac, Ljubo Wiesner, Milan Ogrizović et al.

ANDRIĆ, IVO. "A. G. Matoš." *Vihor* 5 (1914): 89–91. Commemorative remarks delivered to a student audience in Vienna. Somewhat rhetorical.

BARAC, ANTUN. "Matoševa lirika" [Matoš's Poetry]. In *Savremenik* (Beogradski, Izdavačko-grafički Zavod, Belgrade), (1919).

———. "Stihovi A. G. Matoša" [Matoš's Verse]. In *Knjiga eseja* [Essays]. Zagreb, 1924. These two articles, now outdated, pay tribute to Matoš the poet and are written by a well-known professor of literature.

FRANGEŠ, IVO. "Antun Gustav Matoš, 'Jesenje veče'" [Matoš's poem 'Autumn Evening']. *Stilističke studije* [Stylistic Studies]. Zagreb: Naprijed 1959.

———. "Stil Matoševe novelistike" [Matoš's Storytelling Art]. *Rad/JAZU* [Works of the Yugoslav Academy of Science and Art] 333 (1963). Separate edition. Two more recent stylistic evaluations which are at pains to demonstrate sensitivity to language.

KAŠTELAN, JURE. "Lirika A. G. Matoša" [Matoš's Poetry]. *Rad/JAZU* 310 (1957). One famous poet examines another and raises interesting questions.

UJEVIĆ, AUGUSTIN. "Spomen A. G. Matošu" [In Memory of Matoš]. *Savremenik*
(1914).

————. "Em smo Horvati" [We Remain Croats Still]. In *A. G. Matoš—In
Memoriam* (see above).

————. *Sabrana djela.* Vol. 16. Zagreb: Znanje, 1967. Any article by Ujević
is of interest because he parted ways with the master and became a great
poet in his own right. He writes vividly—and negatively, especially in
his *Collected Works.* Usually he had Matoš dead to rights.

Index